NUTMEG

Good COOKING Step by Step

Good
COOKING
Step by Step

HAMLYN
London · New York · Sydney · Toronto

The author and publishers would like to thank The Boots Company for supplying a selection of their merchandise for use in the photographs.

Photography by John Lee, Paul Williams (pages 14-23, 28-29, 38-39, 48-49, 54-57, 62-64, 66-67, 82-83, 90-91, 104-105, 124-125, 156-157, 174-175, 184-185, endpaper) and Roger Philips (pages 166-169, 172-173, 178-181).

Front cover photograph by Paul Kemp
Line drawings by Ann Rees

First published for general circulation 1984 by
The Hamlyn Publishing Group Limited
London · New York · Sydney · Toronto
Astronaut House, Feltham, Middlesex, England
© Copyright The Hamlyn Publishing Group Limited 1979

ISBN 0 600 32430 3

Phototypeset in England by Photocomp Limited, Birmingham
Printed in Italy by New Interlitho, Milan

Contents

Useful Facts and Figures

Notes on metrication

In this book quantities are given in metric and Imperial measures. Exact conversion from Imperial to metric measures does not usually give very convenient working quantities and so the metric measures have been rounded off into units of 25 grams. The table below shows the recommended equivalents.

Ounces	Approx g to nearest whole figure	Recommended conversion to nearest unit of 25
1	28	25
2	57	50
3	85	75
4	113	100/110
5	142	150
6	170	175
7	198	200
8	227	225
9	255	250
10	283	275
11	312	300
12	340	350
13	368	375
14	396	400
15	425	425
16 (1 lb)	454	450
17	482	475
18	510	500
19	539	550
20 (1¼ lb)	567	575

Note: When converting quantities over 20 oz first add the appropriate figures in the centre column, then adjust to the nearest unit of 25. As a general guide, 1 kg (1000 g) equals 2.2 lb or about 2 lb 3 oz. This method of conversion gives good results in nearly all cases, although in certain pastry and cake recipes a more accurate conversion is necessary to produce a balanced recipe.

Liquid measures

The millilitre has been used in this book and the following table gives a few examples.

Imperial	Approx ml to nearest whole figure	Recommended ml
¼ pint	142	150 ml
½ pint	283	300 ml
¾ pint	425	450 ml
1 pint	567	600 ml
1½ pints	851	900 ml
1¾ pints	992	1000 ml (1 litre)

Spoon measures All spoon measures given in this book are level unless otherwise stated.

Can sizes At present, cans are marked with the exact (usually to the nearest whole number) metric equivalent of the Imperial weight of the contents, so we have followed this practice when giving can sizes.

Oven temperatures

The table below gives recommended equivalents.

	°C	°F	Gas Mark
Very cool	110	225	¼
	120	250	½
Cool	140	275	1
	150	300	2
Moderate	160	325	3
	180	350	4
Moderately hot	190	375	5
	200	400	6
Hot	220	425	7
	230	450	8
Very hot	240	475	9

Notes for American and Australian users

In America the 8-oz measuring cup is used. In
Australia metric measures are now used in
conjunction with the standard 250-ml measuring
cup. The Imperial pint, used in Britain and
Australia, is 20 fl oz, while the American pint is
16 fl oz. It is important to remember that the
Australian tablespoon differs from both the British
and American tablespoons; the table below gives a
comparison. The British standard tablespoon, which
has been used throughout this book, holds 17.7 ml,
the American 14.2 ml, and the Australian 20 ml. A
teaspoon holds approximately 5 ml in all three
countries.

British	American	Australian
1 teaspoon	1 teaspoon	1 teaspoon
1 tablespoon	1 tablespoon	1 tablespoon
2 tablespoons	3 tablespoons	2 tablespoons
3½ tablespoons	4 tablespoons	3 tablespoons
4 tablespoons	5 tablespoons	3½ tablespoons

An Imperial/American guide to solid and liquid measures

Solid measures

Imperial	American
1 lb butter or margarine	2 cups
1 lb flour	4 cups
1 lb granulated or castor sugar	2 cups
1 lb icing sugar	3 cups
8 oz rice	1 cup

Liquid measures

Imperial	American
¼ pint liquid	⅔ cup liquid
½ pint	1¼ cups
¾ pint	2 cups
1 pint	2½ cups
1½ pints	3¾ cups
2 pints	5 cups (2½ pints)

Note: WHEN MAKING ANY OF THE RECIPES IN THIS
BOOK, ONLY FOLLOW ONE SET OF MEASURES AS THEY
ARE NOT INTERCHANGEABLE.

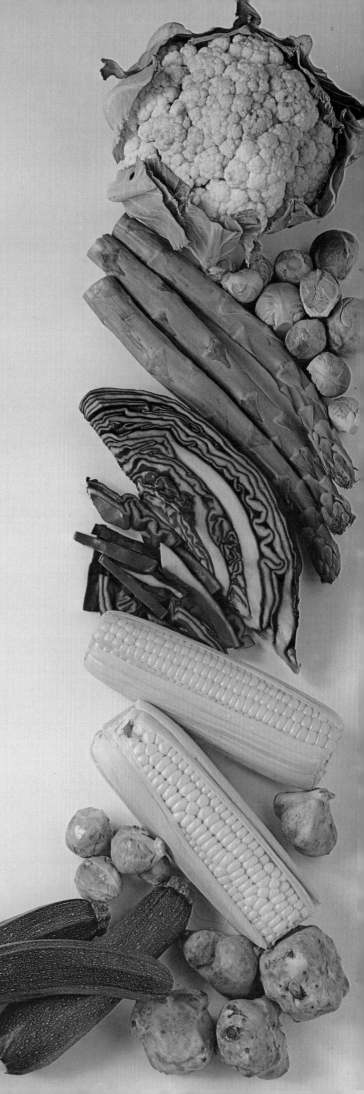

Introduction

I suppose I have been asked on literally thousands of occasions just how does one become a good cook. There are a number of important points to consider in order to achieve this distinction; I believe they are covered in this book.

Firstly you must take a genuine interest in food itself, learn to shop well and recognise when foods are of good quality. This point is covered in the introduction to the various chapters. Pleasure in preparing dishes is helped, I am sure, by interesting recipes. I hope you agree this book contains a good selection of such dishes.

As you become more experienced, develop a critical appreciation of the variance between a perfectly cooked dish and one that is just mediocre. Why the big difference? In most cases the superb dish, whether simple or more complicated, has a clever blending of flavours and the texture of the food is just as it should be. These are points to remember when cooking food itself; taste as you go, adjusting the seasoning and flavours gradually and carefully, so the dish is neither too salt, too sweet or over-powering in taste. Make certain you do not over-cook the ingredients.

Presentation of food is important. It should appear colourful and make you want to eat it which is why we have included so many photographs in this book. They give an idea of how the dish can look when completed and should be a source of inspiration though naturally you will have your own good ideas on garnish and decoration.

Another important factor in becoming a really accomplished cook is to use the right cooking techniques; in other words if a recipe says 'simmer' it is because quicker cooking would probably spoil the food. If the directions stress that 'folding' is the right method of incorporating the ingredients, it indicates that brisker handling could harm the texture. These terms are explained on page 14.

Do not think that becoming a good cook is too difficult for you, it is within everyone's capacity. Enjoy cooking, follow the directions carefully until you feel completely confident, and within a very short time your family and friends will be singing your praises.

No book can be prepared without a great deal of co-operation from other people. I would like to record my appreciation, and thanks, to the home economists who prepared the dishes for the photographs. I owe particular gratitude to Jennifer Feller, Deputy Editor of the Hamlyn Cookery Books, for all her help and hard work.

Marguerite Patten

Cookery Terms

The language of cookery is a specialised one and it makes it easier to follow recipes if you understand the exact meaning of the term.

Bain-marie A dish of water in which the cooking container is placed to prevent curdling or drying.

Bake Cook in the oven without fat. Used for cakes, biscuits, bread and savoury foods.

Bake blind Bake without filling, see Custard tart, page 128.

Baste Spoon fat or liquid over food to keep it moist.

Blanch Whiten certain meats, such as tripe, by putting in cold water then bringing to the boil. Remove the skins from almonds.

Blend Mix ingredients. Can be liquids or solids.

Boil Cook in liquid at 100°C/212°F.

Bouquet garni A bunch of herbs, often parsley, thyme and a bay leaf, tied together with string; or a prepared mixture of herbs in a muslin bag.

Braise Prepare with a rich mirepoix, see page 61.

Casserole Cook in a covered dish in the oven.

Chop Cut food into small pieces. Use a sharp knife and board.

Coat Cover food with flour or brush with egg and coat with crumbs or with a batter.

Consistency The texture of a mixture. A spoon is often used to judge the density.

Cream Mix ingredients, often fat and sugar, to the consistency of whipped cream, see page 132.

Curdle Cause ingredients to separate, either in mixing or cooking.

Decorate Add attractive ingredients to a dish before serving. Usually used for sweet dishes. See Garnish below.

Dice Cut into even cubes.

Dredge Coat lightly with flour or sugar.

Flake Divide into small slivers.

Fold Gently flick ingredients together.

Fry Cook in shallow or deep fat.

Garnish Decorate savoury dishes.

Glaze Give a shiny finish to food by brushing with beaten egg, etc.

Grill Cook under the heat of a grill.

Knead Work dough into a uniform mixture, see page 176.

Knock back Knead dough that has 'proved' until it has returned to its original size, see page 177.

Parboil Partially cook by boiling; do this with parsnips before roasting.

Pare Remove skin or rind.

Poach Cook slowly in liquid, just below boiling point.

Prove Allow yeast dough to rise.

Purée Create a smooth, thick mixture, either by sieving or liquidising.

Roast Cook meat, poultry or vegetables in extra fat or the natural fat of meat, in the oven or over a rotisserie spit.

Roux The mixture of fat and flour in a sauce.

Rub-in A way of incorporating fat and flour, see page 126.

Season 1) Add salt and pepper.
2) Prepare an omelette pan.

Sieve Rub food through a mesh to remove any lumps.

Simmer Cook below boiling point; there should be an occasional bubble on the surface of the liquid.

Sponge A type of light whisked cake.

Steam Cook in the steam rising from boiling water.

Stew Cook in liquid in a covered container, generally at simmering point.

Strain Remove solid food from the liquid, done with a sieve, strainer, muslin or colander.

Toss Turn a pancake. Toss food in fat, often called 'to sauté'.

Whip Beat briskly, i.e. to thicken cream or egg whites.

Whisk See Whip.

Your Kitchen Tools

Just as a competent workman prizes good tools, so a good cook needs first-class equipment. These are the basic tools you will need.

Good knives, etc. for cutting

Cook's knife for cutting, chopping. This is the most 'hard-working' of all knives so worth buying a good one; check it is well balanced.

Small sharp knife for paring fruit and vegetables, plus a potato peeler.

Flexible flat-bladed palette knife.

Bread knife and carving knife, plus a carving fork.

In addition you can add a narrow flexible filleting knife and grapefruit knife.

Chopping board – laminated surfaces are spoiled by food being chopped or cut on these.

Kitchen scissors – invaluable for chopping herbs, removing the rind from bacon, jointing chicken.

For stirring, whisking, etc.

Wooden spoons for creaming, stirring, etc.

Whisk – even if you have an electric whisk a balloon type whisk is invaluable for keeping sauces smooth, for beating cream, etc. If you do not have an electric whisk, then a rotary whisk is extremely efficient.

Standard tablespoon to give correct measurements and to use for more gentle movements than those obtained by a wooden spoon.

For weighing and measuring

Tablespoon – see above.

Standard teaspoon.

Efficient scales – when buying these check they give metric as well as Imperial weights.

Accurate measure for liquid quantities – check it gives metric as well as Imperial measures.

For cooking and food preparation

Flour dredger for shaking flour over the board when making pastry, scones, biscuits, etc.

Grater – buy one of good quality that will not rust. You need this even if you have a slicing and grating attachment on an electric mixer. A Mouli-grater is an excellent utensil for fine grating of cheese, etc.

Mincer – if you have no mincing attachment on an electric mixer or food processor. Make certain it is strong and will take really solid pieces of food.

Sieve – you will need this even if you have a liquidiser (blender) or a food processor to give absolutely smooth purées or strain certain foods. If buying just one choose a nylon, rather than a metal mesh for this will not discolour acid fruits.

Baking sheets or trays – modern non-stick ones seem expensive, but give good results.

Cake tins – of various sizes. Have at least one with a loose base for fragile cakes.

Can-opener – unless you have an attachment on an electric mixer.

Casseroles – of various sizes. You can have saucepans that also serve as casseroles.

Frying pan – check the right type for your hot plate or boiling ring. Choose one with a lid to make a shallow saucepan, also an omelette pan, which could be used for pancakes too.

Pastry brush – for greasing tins, brushing pastry to glaze.

Patty tins – for small cakes or tartlets.

Pie dish with pie funnel.

Roasting tin – generally supplied with the cooker.

Saucepans – choose a range of sizes, but not too small. Check on weight, they should feel well balanced. For certain hot plates the base must be solid. Lids should fit well.

Steamer – one or two tier, for puddings.

Specialised Equipment

There is an almost bewildering array of equipment on the market today. Before making a selection, consider just how they will help you in the preparation of meals for your family and friends.

A Liquidiser (Blender)

This is probably one of the most versatile of electrical gadgets and deservedly popular.

It will take the place of a sieve in most instances, preparing purées and smooth soups. It does not deal entirely with tough skins or hard pips.

A liquidiser can be used for blending or emulsifying ingredients together for mayonnaise, pâtés and spreads.

Dried foods – such as the ingredients for stuffings – cheese and nuts can be chopped in the goblet.

It is excellent for preparing frothy drinks like milk-shakes.

The liquidiser is not a good means of creaming mixtures for cakes and does not whisk egg whites for meringues.

A Food Processor

This appliance can be compared to a liquidiser, for it fulfils many of the same functions. It does however deal with larger quantities of food for pâtés and spreads.

Attachments are included to shred, slice, chop and grate and, in some models, to extract the juice from fruit and vegetables. It is excellent for chopping raw or cooked meat, so takes the place of a mincer.

Cakes, pastry, biscuit and yeast mixtures can be blended in the food processor.

The processor is less good for making true sponges than a mixer and is unsuitable for whisking egg whites.

A Freezer

The advantages of a freezer are numerous and it is considered an essential appliance in many homes.

You can bulk-buy meat, vegetables and other foods and save money; cook in advance and in bulk, so saving time and effort when you are busy.

If used wisely there is always a ready-prepared meal available, just waiting to be heated or defrosted and served cold. You can keep a stock of foods so last-minute shopping is unnecessary.

It is important to wrap foods correctly to keep ingredients in perfect condition. The instruction book with the freezer will give a list of wrappings; these range from foil to heavy-quality polythene bags and boxes.

Maximum storage times are given for prepared recipes. What happens if left too long? The food or dish does not go bad but loses both flavour and texture. It means, therefore, that to enjoy foods from your freezer you should eat them well within the recommended period.

A Slow Cooker (Crock-pot)

Main dishes, some puddings, even some cakes, cooked in a slow cooker can be left unattended for many hours without fear of spoiling or over-cooking. Slow cooking tenderises tougher inexpensive meat very successfully.

The electrical consumption of a slow cooker is comparable to that of an electric light bulb, so it keeps down fuel costs.

This is an ideal appliance for people who like to leave food cooking with little, if any, attention.

A Pressure Cooker

This decreases cooking time very drastically, for example a beef stew that would take approximately $2\frac{1}{2}$ hours slow cooking in a casserole or saucepan, is tenderised and cooked within 15 minutes pressure cooking time on High (15 lb) pressure.

This cooker, which looks like a saucepan, can prepare soups, stocks, vegetables, puddings, a great variety of fish, meat and poultry dishes.

When cooking under pressure, cooking times are reduced due to the build-up of pressure inside the sealed container.

Careful timing is essential when using a pressure cooker. One minute too long could spoil green vegetables.

It is an appliance which is invaluable *if* you use it carefully.

The Microwave Cooker

This, the newest of the electrical appliances, is a revolutionary means of cooking foods within minutes, instead of hours in some cases.

Originally this cooker was only considered of value in catering establishments – to reheat cooked food. This is certainly one of its functions, but there are many others.

Use the cooker to defrost frozen foods quickly and successfully. The microwave cooks a variety of foods, but one cannot say *all* foods are successful. Tough meats will not become tender, unless the model has variable control.

Foods do not brown in the microwave as they do in a conventional cooker, although browning grills are now being incorporated into many models. Browning dishes can also be bought separately.

If you have the kind of family who come into meals at odd times a microwave cooker can make life so very much simpler for you. It cooks fish, certain meat dishes, some puddings, very successfully indeed, and is certainly the best way of reheating food for late-comers.

A Mixer

These range from large models to small compact portable mixers. The mixer rubs-in, whisks, creams, kneads ingredients for cakes, pastry, bread and sponges, whips cream and egg whites.

Many models have a variety of attachments such as slicers and shredders, coffee grinders, mincers, can-openers, juice extractors and separators.

They do not take the place of a liquidiser but the liquidiser goblet can be fixed on to a number of mixers.

Starters

Secrets of Success

Before deciding upon this first course
consider the menu as a whole. Each course
should complement the others in flavour,
colour and appearance. You would not
want every dish creamy in consistency,
highly spiced or based upon fruit.

The meal starter should really be the
cook's last choice, after due consideration
of the main course, then the dessert. If the
main course is substantial or rich in flavour,
choose a light dish as the first course, such
as a perfectly ripe melon or grapefruit.

Cut and decorate melon slices, as illus-
trated. If serving halved melons remove all
the seeds and fill the centres with diced
orange segments, or a scoop of lemon
sorbet, or port wine, and arrange fresh
leaves around the edges of the plates.

Remember that grapefruit is equally good hot or cold. Always cut the segments of the fruit so they are easy to eat. For hot grapefruit, top each prepared half with brown sugar or honey, then about 7 g/¼ oz melted butter, a sprinkling of sherry or rum and a dusting of grated nutmeg or ground cinnamon. Heat in the oven or under the grill until the topping bubbles.

If you would like a more original way of serving cold grapefruit, blend the segments with diced avocado and French dressing (page 100) or with the ingredients in a Prawn Cocktail (page 26).

Serve pâté when you have a relatively light main dish and make it look colourful by garnishing with lemon, lettuce, cucumber and tomato. Cumberland Sauce (page 72) is a little known but excellent accompaniment to meat pâtés.

A Prawn Cocktail is always popular with lovers of shellfish, but its success depends upon a good sauce. This is based on mayonnaise and you will find step-by-step directions on page 26.

The technique employed to make mayonnaise is that of **emulsifying,** i.e. the careful and steady blending together of the egg yolks, or whole eggs in some cases, and the oil.

When once you have learned to make mayonnaise well you can create innumerable recipes for sauces and the popular 'dips', a selection of which are on page 27.

Bacon and Liver Pâté

METRIC/IMPERIAL
675 g/1½ lb pig's liver
225 g/8 oz unsmoked bacon
1 clove garlic or 1 shallot
1 (56-g/2-oz) can anchovy fillets
1 egg
1 egg yolk
½ teaspoon salt
¼ teaspoon black pepper
100 g/4 oz fresh breadcrumbs
1 bay leaf
To line the tin:
175 g/6 oz streaky bacon in thin rashers
To garnish:
slices of cucumber
lettuce

Serves 8

1 Put half the liver into water to cover and simmer until just firm. Put both the cooked and uncooked liver and unsmoked bacon, garlic and anchovies through the mincer twice. Beat the egg and egg yolk together and add with the seasoning and bread-crumbs. Mix very thoroughly. (If a more pronounced onion flavour is liked, add 1 tablespoon grated onion).

2 Lay the bay leaf at the bottom of a 1-kg/2-lb loaf tin or cake tin and line with the thin streaky bacon. Fill with pâté mixture and arrange one or two more thin rashers neatly over the top.

3 Place in a container with hot water reaching at least 2.5 cm/1 inch up the sides of the loaf tin. Cover with a piece of greaseproof paper, without tying it down. Cook in the centre of a moderate oven (180°C, 350°F, Gas Mark 4) for about 1½ hours, removing the paper after 30 minutes.

4 Remove the dish from the oven and put a weighted plate or board on top of the pâté. Leave until cold, then turn out and garnish with cucumber slices and lettuce. Serve with hot toast and butter.

❋ Cool, cover and freeze for up to 1 month.

Prawn Cocktail

METRIC/IMPERIAL
few crisp lettuce leaves
100 g/4 oz peeled prawns or shrimps
slices of lemon to garnish
For the sauce :
3 tablespoons thick mayonnaise
1 tablespoon tomato ketchup or thick
tomato purée
1 tablespoon Worcestershire sauce
2 tablespoons double or single cream
salt and pepper
pinch of celery salt or a little chopped
celery
½ teaspoon finely chopped onion (optional)
squeeze of lemon juice

Serves 4

Shred the lettuce very finely, so it can be eaten with a spoon or small fork, and place in individual glasses. Top with the prawns or shrimps.

To prepare the sauce: Mix all the ingredients together until well blended. Cover the prawns with the sauce and garnish with lemon slices.

Serve with thin slices of brown bread and butter.

Mayonnaise

METRIC/IMPERIAL
2 egg yolks
½ teaspoon dry mustard
¼ teaspoon salt
¼ teaspoon pepper
¼ teaspoon paprika
4 tablespoons vinegar or lemon juice
150 ml/¼ pint salad oil

1 **By hand:** put the egg yolks into a basin with the mustard, salt, pepper and paprika and mix thoroughly. Add 2 tablespoons of vinegar or lemon juice and stir well.

2 Add the oil drop by drop, stirring with a wooden spoon until the mayonnaise is thick and smooth. Do not add too much oil, as this will curdle the mayonnaise. Gradually add the remaining vinegar or lemon juice (if desired) and beat vigorously.

Spiced mayonnaise: add a little grated nutmeg and a few drops of Worcestershire sauce to 150 ml/¼ pint mayonnaise. Serve with potato and vegetable salads.

Mayonnaise Dips

METRIC/IMPERIAL
2 tablespoons French mustard
3 tablespoons mayonnaise
2 tablespoons tomato ketchup
few drops of Worcestershire sauce

Mix all the ingredients together and garnish with a sprig of parsley.

METRIC/IMPERIAL
2-3 rings canned pineapple
3-4 spring onions
2 tablespoons mayonnaise
1 tablespoon lemon juice
grated rind of 1 lemon

Chop the pineapple and onions finely and mix with the other ingredients.

METRIC/IMPERIAL
100 g/4 oz cream cheese
2 tablespoons mayonnaise
few sprigs fresh thyme, finely chopped
few sprigs fresh parsley, finely chopped
few sprigs fresh sage, finely chopped
small bunch fresh chives, chopped

Mix all the ingredients except the chives together. Serve sprinkled with the chopped chives.

3 Using a blender: put the egg yolks, mustard, salt, pepper and paprika in the liquidiser with 2 tablespoons of vinegar or lemon juice. Place the lid on the liquidiser and remove the centre piece. With the liquidiser turned on to a slow speed, pour in the oil in a steady stream until the mixture starts to thicken. At this stage add the remaining vinegar or lemon juice (if desired). Add the remaining oil, increasing the speed.

✳ Do not freeze mayonnaise as it will separate.

Variations
Cheese mayonnaise: cream 50 g/2 oz soft cheese with 2 tablespoons milk. Add 150 ml/¼ pint mayonnaise. Serve with vegetables and salads.
Curry mayonnaise: mix 1-2 teaspoons curry powder with 1-2 tablespoons milk. Stir in 150 ml/¼ pint mayonnaise. Serve with meat or potato salads.
Green mayonnaise: add chopped fresh herbs to the mayonnaise. Serve with fish salads – if mint is used it is excellent with lamb salads.
Horseradish mayonnaise: combine 1 tablespoon horseradish cream with 150 ml/ ¼ pint mayonnaise. Serve with cold beef salad or mackerel or salmon salads.
Lemon mayonnaise: add the grated rind and juice of 1 lemon to 150 ml/¼ pint mayonnaise. Serve with cheese or fish salads.

Soups

Secrets of Success

A good home-made soup is one of the most enjoyable of all foods. Soup makes a good start to a meal, but some of the more sustaining soups in this section can be a light meal in themselves.

A successful soup should be full of flavour. That does not necessarily mean adding a vast number of ingredients, but rather extracting the best flavour from those used.

Most soups start with stock. Wise cooks appreciate the value of this, and on page 30 you will find directions for making various kinds of stock.

Do not over-cook the vegetables in a soup; both colour and flavour will be lost.

Basically three important techniques are used in soup-making:

Sautéeing–in many recipes onions, or other foods, are tossed in shallow fat at the beginning of the cooking process. This gives a richness of flavour. It is generally very important that the foods are not over-browned during this stage, as this would spoil the appearance of the soup.

Simmering–in most soups the foods are simmered steadily in the stock. This ensures that they are adequately softened and you achieve a subtle blending of flavours. Sometimes eggs and/or cream, or a creamy sauce, are mixed with the rest of the ingredients and simmering is essential to prevent the mixture curdling.

Thickening–in certain soups the liquid needs to be thickened. After adding the flour mixture cook adequately so there is no taste of under-cooked flour.

Although not a basic cooking process the technique I would highlight with soup-making is **flavouring.** In addition to a good stock, and the right choice of ingredients, make use of herbs and seasonings. Always remember to check the flavour at least twice during the cooking of a soup–firstly when all the ingredients are added and secondly before serving. *Never over-season*, as people's liking for salt and pepper varies a great deal.

Making Stock

Many soups need stock to give additional flavour. When the recipe specifies a brown stock this is made by simmering bones or shin of beef, lamb or game in water to cover for several hours, or cook for 1 hour in a pressure cooker at High (15 lb) pressure. Vegetables and herbs can be added. A white stock is made in the same way, but using bones of veal, chicken or turkey. If home-made stock is not available, substitute stock cubes. Stock is a highly perishable liquid, especially if vegetables have been used, so store carefully; re-boil every other day, even when kept in a refrigerator. Stock freezes well.

A good soup is full of flavour and you obtain this by the wise use of seasoning (not just ordinary salt and pepper, but celery salt, paprika or cayenne) and by the generous use of suitable herbs. Yeast extract can be added and will not only increase the vitamin content but will give an interesting taste as well.

Types of Soup

Soups can be made from most vegetables, so you can plan a variety of dishes through-out the year, based upon the vegetables available. You can choose a clear soup with diced vegetables; a purée soup, where the vegetables are sieved or liquidised; or a creamed soup, where the vegetables are blended with cream or a creamy sauce.

Broths and chowders are both thick soups and could be served for a supper dish. Meat, fish and vegetables are all used to make this type of soup.

Clear soups are ideal when you are not particularly hungry or when trying to lose weight.

To Freeze Soups

Stock freezes well. Pour the liquid into waxed or polythene containers, allowing 1 cm/½ inch 'head-room'. If you prefer to use polythene bags, stand these in a firm container (such as a sugar carton), pour in the soup, seal, freeze, then remove the bag from the carton; this gives you a neat pack for easy storage. A more 'space-saving' method of freezing concentrated stock is to pour this into ice-cube trays, freeze, then store the cubes in suitable containers. Use within 3 months. Frozen purée or meat soups should be used within the same length of time.

Consommé

METRIC/IMPERIAL
350 g/12 oz shin of beef
1.15 litres/2 pints good stock
salt and pepper
1 onion
small piece celery
1 sprig of parsley
1 bay leaf
1 carrot
2 teaspoons sherry (optional)

Serves 3-4

Cut the meat into small pieces and put these into the saucepan, together with all the other ingredients except the sherry.

Bring to the boil and remove any scum, then simmer very gently for 1 hour and strain through several thicknesses of muslin. Add sherry if desired.

To clear a consommé, put in a stiffly beaten egg white and clean egg shell and gently simmer again for 20 minutes, then re-strain. Any tiny particles left in the stock adhere to the egg white and shell.

Minestrone Soup

METRIC/IMPERIAL
75 g/3 oz haricot beans
900 ml/1½ pints white stock
1 large onion
2 tablespoons oil
1 clove garlic, crushed
50 g/2 oz bacon, diced
1 stick celery
1 carrot
225 g/8 oz tomatoes
salt and pepper
100 g/4 oz cabbage
50 g/2 oz macaroni or vermicelli
To garnish:
chopped parsley
grated Parmesan cheese

Serves 4

Soak the beans overnight in the stock.

Chop the onion very finely and toss in the hot oil for 2 minutes. Add the crushed clove of garlic and the diced bacon and cook for a few minutes. Put in the soaked haricot beans and the liquid in which they were soaked. Cover the pan and simmer gently for 1½ hours.

Finely chop the celery, peel and dice the carrot and peel the tomatoes. Add to the soup with seasoning and cook for 15 minutes. Shred the cabbage very finely and break the pasta into short lengths. Add to the soup with the cabbage and continue cooking for 15-20 minutes until tender.

Taste the soup and re-season if necessary. Top with a generous amount of chopped parsley and grated cheese.

❋ Freezes well for 1 month. After this time pasta becomes over-soft.

Cream Of Tomato Soup

METRIC/IMPERIAL
450 g/1 lb ripe tomatoes
1 onion
1 carrot
1 stick celery
2 rashers bacon
25 g/1 oz butter (optional)
600 ml/1 pint white stock
salt and pepper
1 bouquet garni
25 g/1 oz butter
25 g/1 oz flour
450 ml/¾ pint milk

Serves 4

1 Peel and chop the tomatoes and onion and peel and grate the carrot. Chop the celery and bacon. Heat the bacon in a pan, add the butter then add the vegetables and toss well. Do not allow the bacon or onion to brown.

2 Add the stock, seasoning and bouquet garni, cover the soup and simmer gently for approximately 35 minutes.

3 Make a thin white sauce using the remaining ingredients: melt the butter, add the flour and cook, stirring, for 1 minute. Add the milk and stir in well. Heat until thickened. Sieve the cooked vegetables to a purée.

4 Reheat the tomato purée and whisk in the hot sauce. Do not let the sauce or purée boil. Serve immediately.

❊ It is better to freeze the tomato purée, then blend with the sauce when reheating.

Cucumber Purée Soup

METRIC/IMPERIAL
1 large or 2 medium cucumbers
1 onion
small piece celery
450 ml/¾ pint white stock
25 g/1 oz butter
25 g/1 oz flour
300 ml/½ pint milk
salt and pepper
chopped parsley to garnish

Serves 3-4

Peel the cucumber, leaving a little skin on to give a green colour. Too much skin left on gives a bitter taste. Chop the cucumber and peel and chop the onion. Chop the celery and mix with the cucumber and onion. If celery is not obtainable, chicory or celeriac can be used instead. Put into a pan with the stock and simmer until tender. Rub through a sieve.

Meanwhile make a white sauce with the butter, flour and milk: melt the butter, add the flour and cook, stirring, for 1 minute. Stir in the milk and heat until thick, stirring continuously.

Add the cucumber purée to the sauce and reheat. Season well. A little lemon juice can be added when heated but do not boil again. Garnish with chopped parsley.

✳ It is better to freeze the cucumber purée, then blend with the sauce when reheating.

Dried Pea Soup

METRIC/IMPERIAL
225 g/8 oz dried split peas
1.15 litres/2 pints bacon stock
2 onions
1 carrot
1 turnip
salt and pepper
1 sprig of mint
1 teaspoon sugar

Serves 4-6

Soak the peas overnight in the stock. Peel and chop the onions, carrot and turnip. Add to the peas and stock in a pan. Add the seasoning and mint and simmer for 1¼-1½ hours.

Either rub through a sieve, beat until very smooth, or liquidise.

Pour the purée back into the pan, add sugar to taste and adjust the seasoning. Reheat gently and serve.

✳ Freeze for 3 months.

Mulligatawny Soup

METRIC/IMPERIAL
1 apple
1 large carrot
2 onions
50 g/2 oz fat or dripping
25 g/1 oz flour
1 tablespoon curry powder
1.15 litres/2 pints lamb stock
1 tablespoon chutney
25 g/1 oz sultanas
pinch of sugar
salt and pepper
little lemon juice or vinegar

Serves 4-6

Peel the apple and vegetables and chop into tiny pieces. Toss in the hot dripping, then work in the flour and curry powder. Add the stock, bring to the boil and cook until thickened. Add the remaining ingredients and cook together for about 45 minutes-1 hour.

Rub through a sieve and return to the pan to reheat. Taste, adjusting seasoning if necessary, and add a little extra sugar or lemon juice if required.

❄ Freeze for 3 months.

Welsh Leek Soup

METRIC/IMPERIAL
1 large onion
6 medium leeks
50 g/2 oz butter
900 ml/1½ pints chicken stock
2 medium potatoes
1 tablespoon chopped parsley
2 egg yolks
150 ml/¼ pint double cream or milk
salt and pepper
chopped chives or chopped parsley to
garnish

Serves 4

Peel the onion and chop with the leeks. Fry in the butter until golden but not too brown. Add the stock and season well.

Peel and chop the potatoes and add to the soup with the parsley. Simmer for 30 minutes.

Rub through a fine sieve and return to the pan. Blend the egg yolks with the cream, add to the soup and cook *without boiling* for a few minutes. Adjust the seasoning if necessary and serve topped with chives or parsley.

Watercress Soup

METRIC/IMPERIAL
100 g/4 oz watercress
1 tablespoon corn oil
2 teaspoons yeast extract
600 ml/1 pint water or stock
15 g/½ oz cornflour
5 tablespoons milk or single cream
salt and pepper

Serves 3-4

Wash the watercress well. Reserving a few sprigs for the garnish, remove the leaves from the stalks of the remainder and chop finely. Sauté gently for 2-3 minutes in the heated oil. Add the yeast extract and the water. Bring to the boil, stirring, then simmer for about 5 minutes. Sieve or liquidise if required.

Mix the cornflour and milk smoothly, add to the purée and cook for 3 minutes, stirring all the time. Season to taste. Garnish with a sprig of watercress.

✳ It is better to freeze the watercress mixture and add the thickening when reheating.

White Fish Soup

METRIC/IMPERIAL
350 g/12 oz white fish
225 g/8 oz fish trimmings (skin and bones)
1.15 litres/2 pints water
1 large onion or 2 leeks
40 g/1½ oz margarine
40 g/1½ oz flour
150 ml/¼ pint milk
salt and pepper
1 teaspoon chopped parsley

Serves 4-6

Wash and clean the fish and trimmings. Simmer the trimmings in the water for 10 minutes and strain. Place the fish in a pan with the stock. Peel and slice the onion or leeks and add to the fish. Bring to the boil and skim well. Cook gently for 10 minutes. Lift out the fish and flake. Cook the stock for 30 minutes longer. Strain the stock and rinse the pan.

Melt the margarine, add the flour and cook, without colouring, for a few minutes. Add the stock and milk and cook until boiling, stirring continuously. Add the flaked fish, season and boil gently for 5 minutes. Add the chopped parsley and serve.

✳ Use within 2 months.

Fish Dishes

Secrets of Success

Since fresh fish is a highly perishable food, great care must be taken in buying and storing it before cooking.

To judge if white, oily, freshwater and smoked fish are fresh look for bright shiny skin or scales, bright eyes and firm-looking bodies. Stale fish has a definite smell of ammonia.

Shellfish is fresh if bright in colour; if you pull out the tails of prawns or lobsters these should 'spring back'.

Cook as soon as possible after purchase and keep in the refrigerator for the short time before cooking.

Commercially frozen fish should be stored as recommended on the packet. If preparing fresh fish for freezing you must ensure it is absolutely fresh and in first class condition, then wrap it carefully. When frozen fish has defrosted it must be treated as perishable fresh fish.

The recommended maximum storage time in the freezer for uncooked fish is as follows:
White and freshwater fish up to 6 months; *oily fish* up to 3 months; *smoked fish* up to 3 months.
Crab and lobster should be cooked before

freezing, other shellfish such as scampi can be frozen uncooked for up to 1 month.

One of the most important points in fish cookery is not to over-cook. Timing varies according to the method of cooking and the shape and thickness of the fish. The best test is to insert the tip of a knife into the fish when you think it is cooked and see if the fish *just* forms flakes. Cooked white fish changes in colour from being translucent to milky-white.

The methods of cooking used in this chapter are:

Baking – take care the fish is kept moist and does not over-cook in the oven.

Boiling – really an incorrect title since fish must be **poached** in simmering liquid, not boiled.

Frying – check the temperature of the oil or fat is correct before adding the fish.

Grilling – always preheat the grill so the fish starts to cook quickly. Keep the fish well basted with butter, oil or fat.

Steaming – this is a method of cooking fish covered over boiling water, generally with a little liquid and butter. Steaming can be carried out with the fish between two plates over a pan of boiling water.

To Fillet Fish

Fish is easier to serve when it has been filleted, i.e. when the fish is taken off the bone. This is generally done by the fishmonger if asked, but it is worthwhile knowing how to do it. The method depends upon the type of fish – flat fish, for example, can be made into four small, or two large fillets. Always choose a sharp knife, one with a point so this may be inserted under the flesh. If the tip of the knife is dipped in salt it has a better cutting edge; naturally this salt must be rinsed off the fish.

To fillet flat fish

1 Cut off the fins using a sharp knife. Working from the head to the tail, make a deep cut down the backbone on the back of the fish (this is the side with the dark skin).

2 Insert the tip of the knife at the head end of the incision and carefully loosen the flesh away from the backbone with short sharp strokes. Fold the fillet back gently with your fingers as you work. Do not pull or hurry or flesh will be left on the backbone. Turn the fish the other way and repeat the process, this time working from the tail end. Turn the fish over and do the same on the white side to give four fillets.

To fillet round fish

1 Cut off the head using a sharp knife. Cut along the backbone from the head towards the tail.

2 Insert a sharp knife at an angle to the backbone with the blade towards the tail. Slice the flesh gradually from the bone. Continue away from the bone until the whole fillet is freed. Cut the fillet off at the tail. Lift the backbone away from the second fillet using the tip of the knife and cut off the tail.

※ If freezing filleted fish, separate each fillet with greaseproof or waxed paper then wrap. Use within 4 months.

Flour Coating

METRIC/IMPERIAL
25-40 g/1-1½ oz flour
salt and pepper

Wash and dry the fish thoroughly with kitchen paper. This makes certain the flour will adhere to it. Season the flour and place on either a piece of greaseproof paper or on a flat surface. Press the fish on to the flour on one side, turn and do the same with the second side. Make sure the fish is completely covered; then lift on to a clean plate.

Egg and Breadcrumbs

METRIC/IMPERIAL
15-25 g/½-1 oz flour
salt and pepper
1 egg
2 teaspoons water
3-4 tablespoons raspings

To coat 4 portions of fish

Wash and dry the fish well on kitchen paper. Coat the fish with flour as above. Sometimes this step is omitted, but you will have a more even coating of egg and crumbs if flour is used first. Blend the egg and water together, then either put the fish into the egg and turn it with a spoon and knife or with 2 knives, or leave the fish on a plate and brush the egg over one side of the fish, turn and brush the second side. Whichever method is used, thoroughly coat the fish.

Put the crisp breadcrumbs either on to another plate or square of kitchen or greaseproof paper, or into a greaseproof paper bag. Lift the fish on to the crumbs, if on a plate or square of paper, and press firmly against them so they coat one side; then turn with 2 knives and coat the second side. Press the crumbs very firmly against

the fish with a broad-bladed palette knife, to make certain they stick firmly and do not fall off and burn during cooking. A paper bag is the quickest and easiest way for coating but it sometimes spoils the shape of the fish unless used very carefully. Drop the fish into the crumbs in the bag and shake up and down gently. This is particularly suitable for small portions of cod fillets or steaks of fish or scampi. Lift the coated fish out of the bag and press the crumbs hard against the fish with a palette knife. The fish is then ready to fry.

❊ It is a good idea to coat some fish before freezing. Open freeze then wrap. Use within 3 months.

Batter Coating

METRIC/IMPERIAL
100 g/4 oz flour
pinch of salt
1 egg
150 ml/¼ pint milk*
flour for coating
salt and pepper
*for a thinner coating batter, add 1-2 extra tablespoons milk

To coat 4-6 portions of fish

Sift the flour with the salt, add the egg and beat well, then gradually beat in the milk. Milk and water could be used for a more economical coating.

Coat the fish with flour seasoned with salt and pepper then dip the fish into the batter. Lift out with a fork and spoon and hold suspended over the batter so that any surplus may drop back into the bowl. This saves making any mess as you put the fish into the fat. It also avoids too thick a coating. Use the smaller percentage of milk for rather solid pieces of fish such as cod, and the thinner batter, i.e. the larger quantity of milk, for thinner pieces of fish.

❊ Batter-coated fish is not suitable for freezing.

Whiting with French Mustard Sauce

METRIC/IMPERIAL
4 whiting
salt and pepper
2 small shallots
1 tablespoon French mustard
4 tablespoons dry white wine
juice of $\frac{1}{2}$ lemon
25 g/1 oz butter
1 tablespoon finely chopped parsley
sprigs of parsley to garnish

Serves 4

Arrange the fish in a buttered ovenproof dish and season to taste. Peel the shallots, chop very finely and scatter over the fish. Blend the mustard and wine together and pour over the fish. Cover and bake in a moderate oven (180°C, 350°F, Gas Mark 4) for 20-40 minutes, until the fish is thoroughly cooked.

Pour the cooking liquor off into a saucepan, stir in the lemon juice and heat for 2-3 minutes, stirring continuously to reduce the liquid. Stir in the butter and chopped parsley and pour over the prepared fish. Garnish with sprigs of parsley.

Hake Pimiento

METRIC/IMPERIAL
15 g/$\frac{1}{2}$ oz butter
2 onions
900 g/2 lb hake, cut into 4 cutlets
salt and pepper
1 large green pepper
2 (142-ml/5-fl oz) cartons natural yogurt

Serves 4

Grease an ovenproof dish with the butter. Peel the onions and blanch for about 10 minutes in boiling water. Cut the onions into rings and arrange on the bottom of the dish. Place the fish on top and season well.

Remove the seeds from the green pepper, cut into thin rings and arrange on the fish. Pour the yogurt over and bake for 25-40 minutes, depending on thickness, in a moderate oven (180°C, 350°F, Gas Mark 4). This is also extremely good made with halibut.

❋ Use within 2 months.

Mackerel in Foil

METRIC/IMPERIAL
4 mackerel
salt and pepper
2 firm tomatoes
1 lemon
4 sprigs of parsley
25 g/1 oz butter

Serves 4

Clean the fish and remove the heads. Season well and lay each fish on a piece of buttered foil. Cut the tomatoes and lemon into slices and arrange alternate slices on each fish. Place a large sprig of parsley on top and dot with butter.

Fold the foil up and seal into neat parcels. Place on a baking tray and bake in a moderate oven (180°C, 350°F, Gas Mark 4) for 25-30 minutes. The fish may be served in the foil or transferred to a serving dish, together with the juices formed during the cooking.

✳ Use within 2 months.

Fish and Chips with Fried Parsley

METRIC/IMPERIAL
For the chips:
675 g/1½ lb potatoes
oil or fat for frying
For the fish:
4 portions of cod or plaice
flour, or egg and breadcrumbs, or batter
to coat
oil or fat for frying
parsley to garnish

Serves 4

1 Peel the potatoes and cut into long fingers. Wash these in cold water and dry well. Heat the oil to 180°C/350°F. Test the heat of the oil by dropping in a small cube of bread. The oil is hot enough when the bread turns golden in colour, in about 1 minute. Do not overheat the oil or it will burn before cooking the food.

2 Put enough chips in the frying basket to quarter-fill it. Lower the basket slowly into the oil, watching to see there is no danger of its overflowing. Cook the chips for about 3-5 minutes, or until cooked but not brown. Tip the chips on to a plate until nearly ready to serve the meal.

3 Coat the fish according to taste with flour, egg and breadcrumbs or batter. Test the oil and when it is hot enough, lower the empty basket into it.

4 Lower each piece of fish into the oil by hand to avoid its sticking to the basket. As soon as the fish is in the pan, lower the heat. Never overfill the frying basket. Cook the fish for 3-6 minutes according to thickness. Remove the fish with the basket. Drain for a minute over the pan and turn the fish on to crumpled kitchen paper to drain.

5 Return the chips to the basket. When the oil is hot enough, lower the basket into the oil and cook for a further 2 minutes until crisp and brown. (If frozen chips are used, there is no need to cook them twice.)

6 Wash and dry the parsley and select perfect sprigs. Fry for a few seconds in the hot oil. The parsley should still be green and very crisp. Garnish the fish with slices of lemon and fried parsley and serve with the chips.

Trout Grenobloise

METRIC/IMPERIAL
4 trout
150 g/5 oz butter
50 g/2 oz mushrooms
juice of ½ lemon
2 tablespoons coarse fresh breadcrumbs
To garnish:
slices of lemon
sprigs of parsley

Serves 4

Clean the trout and wipe dry.

Melt the butter in a large pan and fry the trout steadily until cooked, about 10 minutes, turning to cook the other side.

Meanwhile clean and finely chop the mushrooms. When the trout is cooked, remove from the pan and add the lemon juice, mushrooms and breadcrumbs to the remaining butter. Fry for a few minutes and arrange around the cooked trout on a heated serving dish. Garnish with slices of lemon and sprigs of parsley.

✳ Use within 2 months.

Goujons Meunière

METRIC/IMPERIAL
4 large fillets of sole
75 g/3 oz butter
salt and pepper
1 teaspoon lemon juice
2 teaspoons chopped parsley
few capers (optional)
wedges of lemon to garnish

Serves 4

Slice each fillet in half and cut each half lengthways into three or four strips.

Heat the butter, add the goujons and cook for about 4 minutes. Remove the fish and continue to cook the butter until it is

dark brown. Add seasoning, lemon juice, parsley and capers and pour over the goujons. Serve garnished with wedges of lemon.

This recipe can also be made using scampi.

NOTE Do not freeze; serve as soon as cooked.

Cod Provençale

METRIC/IMPERIAL
1 medium onion
1 clove garlic
350 g/12 oz tomatoes
450–575 g/1–1¼ lb skinned cod fillet
25 g/1 oz flour
salt and pepper
oil for frying
1 teaspoon chopped fresh herbs
black olives to garnish (optional)

Serves 4

Peel and slice the onion and crush the garlic. Peel the tomatoes, remove the seeds and slice. Cut the fish into 5-cm/2-inch squares, then roll in the flour seasoned with salt and pepper.

Heat a little oil in a frying pan, then fry the fish quickly until golden brown on both sides for about 8 minutes. Drain, arrange in a shallow serving dish and keep hot.

Strain off the surplus oil, leaving at least a tablespoon in the pan. Fry the onion until tender, then add the garlic, tomato and herbs. Toss quickly over a brisk heat for 2-3 minutes. Season to taste and add the olives if used. Reheat and pour over the fish, or serve as an accompaniment.

❋ Freezes well for 2 months.

Grilled Fish

METRIC/IMPERIAL
butter or oil
4 large or 8 small fillets of white fish,
or 4 thick fish steaks
salt and pepper
1 teaspoon lemon juice

Serves 4

Brush the grid of the grill pan with a little melted butter or oil before cooking, so the fish does not stick, or put buttered foil over the grid, which makes it easier to clean the grill pan and grid.

Brush the fish with a little melted butter or oil before cooking and season lightly. A squeeze of lemon juice gives extra flavour. Alternatively, place a pat of butter on each fillet.

For grilling thin fillets of fish – plaice, sole, whiting – allow approximately 4 minutes cooking time, turning the heat down after the first 2-3 minutes if desired.

For thicker fish, grill quickly for 2-3 minutes first on one side then on the other, to seal in flavour, then reduce the heat for a further 3-4 minutes, brushing the fish once or twice with melted butter or oil. When turning the fish, use a fish slice or broad-bladed palette knife so it does not break.

Mushrooms and halved tomatoes can be cooked in the bottom of the grill pan at the same time.

NOTE This is an excellent way to cook frozen fish.

Parsley or Maître d'Hôtel Butter

METRIC/IMPERIAL
1 teaspoon lemon juice
1-2 teaspoons chopped parsley
salt and pepper
50 g/2 oz butter

Serves 4

Work the lemon juice, parsley and seasoning into the butter.

Form into a neat block and chill – if possible leave in the refrigerator so that it becomes very firm.

Cut into neat pieces and put on the fish just before serving.

❋ Wrap well and freeze for 3 months.

Grilled Plaice with Savoury Butter

METRIC/IMPERIAL
4 large or 8 small fillets of plaice
watercress to garnish
For the butter :
1 clove garlic, crushed (optional)
grated rind of 1 lemon
pinch of cayenne
pinch of celery salt
salt and pepper
75 g/3 oz butter

Serves 4

First make the butter. Combine all the flavourings with the butter and mix well. As none of this should be wasted it is a good idea to put one-third of the savoury butter into the grill pan itself.

Arrange the plaice in the grill pan. Top with the remainder of the butter and spread evenly over the fillets. Grill for about 4 minutes, depending on thickness. Do not overcook. Put the fish on a warmed serving dish, pour over the butter and garnish with watercress.

Sole au Gratin

METRIC/IMPERIAL
4 large or 8 small fillets of sole
little melted butter or oil
For the cheese sauce :
25 g/1 oz butter or margarine
25 g/1 oz flour
300 ml/½ pint milk
75-100 g/3-4 oz cheese, grated
little made mustard
For the topping :
25 g/1 oz cheese, grated
1 tablespoon fresh breadcrumbs
15 g/½ oz butter

Serves 4

Brush the sole with a little melted butter or oil and grill until tender. Alternatively, skin the fillets of sole and carefully roll up from head to tail. Secure with wooden cocktail sticks and place in a well greased ovenproof dish. Brush with melted butter or oil and cover the dish with foil. Bake in a moderate oven (180°C, 350°F, Gas Mark 4) for 25-30 minutes. While the sole is cooking, prepare the cheese sauce (see page 84).

Arrange the grilled fillets in an ovenproof dish and pour over the sauce. Or pour the sauce over the baked fish.

Mix the grated cheese and breadcrumbs together and sprinkle over the fish and sauce. Dot the top with butter and brown under a hot grill for 1-2 minutes.

✳ Can be frozen for 2 months.

Cod Duglêrê

METRIC/IMPERIAL
1 medium onion
15 g/½ oz butter
3 tomatoes
2 teaspoons chopped parsley
2 tablespoons white wine or cider
150 ml/¼ pint water
450-675 g/1-1½ lb frozen cod steaks
parsley to garnish
For the sauce:
15 g/½ oz butter
15 g/½ oz flour

Serves 4

Peel and chop the onion, melt the butter and fry the onion without browning until soft. Peel the tomatoes and remove the seeds. Add the tomatoes, parsley, wine or cider and water to the onion and place the cod steaks in the mixture.

Poach the mixture very gently for 15-20 minutes. Meanwhile melt the butter in another pan and stir in the flour. Remove the fish from the mixture on to a heated serving dish. Add the tomato and wine mixture to the sauce and bring to the boil, stirring until the sauce is thickened. Pour over the fish and serve garnished with parsley.

Jugged Kippers

Place 4 pairs of kippers in a heatproof jug or other container. Pour in enough fast boiling water to cover. Cover the jug and let it stand for 5 minutes in a hot place (beside the hot plates on the stove, for instance).

Remove the fish and drain. Serve with a pat of butter on top of each. *Serves 4.*

Poached Salmon in Court Bouillon

METRIC/IMPERIAL
575-675 g/1¼-1½ lb fresh salmon
salt and pepper
For the court bouillon:
1 onion, peeled and sliced
600 ml/1 pint water or fish stock and a
little wine
2 teaspoons lemon juice
few peppercorns
1 teaspoon salt
1 bouquet garni
To garnish:
slices of cucumber
slices of lemon
sprigs of parsley

Serves 4

Arrange the salmon on a piece of oiled paper, season well and wrap into a neat parcel. Tie securely and put into a saucepan with all the ingredients for the court bouillon, making sure the court bouillon covers the fish.

Bring slowly to the boil and simmer gently, allowing 10 minutes per 450 g/ per lb. Leave to stand until cold. Remove from the cooking liquid and garnish with slices of cucumber, lemon and sprigs of parsley. Serve with new potatoes.

Another way of cooking relatively small pieces of salmon is to bring the water to the boil as above, then remove the pan from the heat. Cover the pan tightly and leave the fish in the water until it is cold. This method is excellent if wishing to serve the fish cold, for there is no possibility of its being overcooked and dry.

❋ Cooked salmon can be frozen for 2 months, uncooked salmon for 4 months.

Fish Salad

METRIC/IMPERIAL
For the dressing :
1 small onion
1 tablespoon dry mustard
1 tablespoon sugar
1 tablespoon lemon juice
grated rind of 1 lemon
5 tablespoons wine vinegar
pinch of cayenne pepper
pinch of salt
few drops of Tabasco sauce
2 tablespoons chopped fresh dill, fennel or parsley
For the salad :
350 g/12 oz white fish, cooked
50 g/2 oz peeled prawns
100 g/4 oz cooked or canned peas
2 eggs, hard-boiled and sliced
1 medium beetroot, cooked and diced
1 crisp lettuce
few unpeeled prawns to garnish

Serves 4-6

Crush the onion and use only the juice. Make the dressing by blending all the ingredients for the dressing together in a basin or by shaking them together in a screw-topped jar.

Flake the fish and mix with the prawns and the sauce. If wished, a little less of the sharp sauce may be used to give a slightly less moist salad.

Add the peas, sliced eggs and diced beetroot. Pile this mixture neatly on to a bed of crisp lettuce. Garnish with prawns. Serve chilled.

Soused Herrings or Mackerel

METRIC/IMPERIAL
4 large or 8 small herrings or mackerel
1 small apple
1 small onion
1 teaspoon pickling spice
1 teaspoon sweet spice
$\frac{1}{2}$ teaspoon salt
1 teaspoon sugar
150 ml/$\frac{1}{4}$ pint water
150 ml/$\frac{1}{4}$ pint vinegar
2 bay leaves

Serves 4

Split the herrings and take out the backbones. Roll the herrings and arrange in a covered casserole. Slice the apple, peel and slice the onion and add to the casserole with all the other ingredients. Cook in a cool oven (150°C, 300°F, Gas Mark 2) for 1 hour.

Leave until quite cold. Serve with lettuce, potato and beetroot salads.

❋ Freeze for up to 6 weeks.

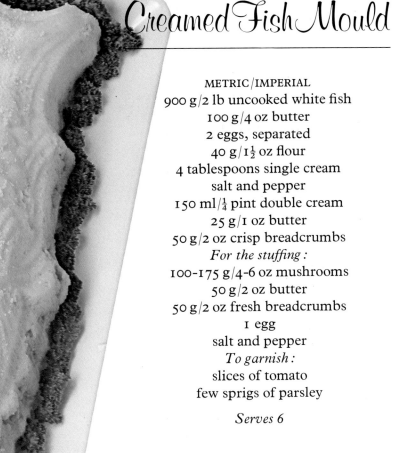

Creamed Fish Mould

METRIC/IMPERIAL
900 g/2 lb uncooked white fish
100 g/4 oz butter
2 eggs, separated
40 g/1½ oz flour
4 tablespoons single cream
salt and pepper
150 ml/¼ pint double cream
25 g/1 oz butter
50 g/2 oz crisp breadcrumbs
For the stuffing:
100-175 g/4-6 oz mushrooms
50 g/2 oz butter
50 g/2 oz fresh breadcrumbs
1 egg
salt and pepper
To garnish:
slices of tomato
few sprigs of parsley

Serves 6

Remove all the bones and skin from the fish. Flake the flesh and pound well. Gradually work the butter into the fish.

Add the egg yolks, flour and single cream gradually to the fish mixture. If the mixture shows signs of curdling, place the bowl of mixture over hot water, beat until smooth and season well.

Lightly whip the double cream and whisk the egg whites until stiff. Fold these into the fish mixture.

Butter a 1.75-litre/3-pint fish mould, coat with the crumbs and pour half of the mixture into this.

Prepare the stuffing. Finely chop the mushrooms and fry in the butter. Add the breadcrumbs, egg and seasoning. Spread this over the fish in the mould and cover with the remaining mixture. Put greased foil over the mixture.

Bake in a cool oven (150°C, 300°F, Gas Mark 2) for 1½ hours until firm. Cool, turn out and garnish with tomato and parsley. Serve cold with salads.

✳ Freezes well for 2 months.

Meat and Poultry

Secrets of Success

Meat and poultry are excellent sources of protein and are extremely adaptable in cooking.

Learn to recognise the various cuts of meat and choose the right cut for each cooking process; you will find more information about this on pages 56-57.

Buy meat and poultry from a butcher or supermarket where you know there are high standards of hygiene and where meat is properly 'hung'; this makes a great deal of difference to the tenderness and flavour. Lean beef is generally bright red, but do not expect it always to be exactly the same colour; the length of time since the joint was cut makes a difference. The fat should be creamy white. Lamb has dull red lean and very white firm fat. Pork should have pale pink lean, but very firm white fat. Veal, of course, has little fat, but any that it has should be firm and white and the lean very pale pink and firm. Bacon and ham must look pleasantly moist.

Good quality young poultry is firm in texture, with pliable breastbones and 'meaty' breasts.

If buying meat for freezing, wrap well and store for the following maximum times: *Beef and lamb* up to 9 months; *pork* up to 6 months; *veal* up to 4 months; *smoked bacon and salted (cured) meat* up to 3 months, providing the bacon has been vacuum packed.

When the meat is cut into smaller pieces reduce the storage time, e.g. minced meat should be used within 3 months, steaks and chops within 6 months. I believe the flavour suffers if stored any longer.

Chicken and game can be frozen for 1 year, turkey, goose and duck up to 8 months, but the giblets should then be packed separately and used within 3 months.

The basic methods of cooking meat and poultry are:

Baking – in pies and savoury dishes. Time the cooking in the oven carefully and be sure the meat or poultry does not become dry.

Boiling – the term given when cooking salted meats; it is not really correct. Having brought the liquid to boiling point, the temperature should be reduced, so the liquid simmers gently. Too rapid cooking toughens meat.

Braising–produces a richer result than stewing. True braising means first browning the food, then cooking above a small quantity of liquid and a bed of savoury ingredients, known as a 'mirepoix'.

Frying–only suitable for prime pieces of meat or for made-up dishes such as rissoles. Check that the food cooks quickly on the outside to brown, then lower the heat to make sure the centre is tender.

Grilling–preheat the grill, except when cooking bacon, as too great a heat makes the bacon fat curl and burn. Always keep lean meat or poultry well basted.

Roasting–the most popular method of cooking joints and poultry. There are two recommended temperatures at which to roast, and information on a wise choice is given on pages 70-71.

Stewing – cooking gently in liquid. This is where cheaper cuts of meat can be tenderised and made delicious. Never cook too quickly.

Know Your Cuts

	Cut	Use
Beef	Aitch-bone	roast (best), pickle, boil
	Bladebone	stew, braise
	Brisket	roast (best), stew, braise
	Chuck (skirt)	stew, braise
	Clod	stock, soup
	Entrecôte	grill, fry
	Fillet	roast, grill, fry
	Flank	stew, braise, boil, pickle, stock
	Marrowbone	stock, soup
	Neck	stock, soup
	Oxtail	casserole, stock, soup
	Ribs	roast
	Rump	roast, grill, fry
	Shin (leg)	boil, pickle, stock, soup
	Silverside	pickle, boil
	Sirloin	roast, grill, fry
	Topside	braise, roast
	(Leg of mutton cut)	stew, braise
Lamb, mutton	Best end of neck (lamb)	roast
	Breast (stuffed, rolled)	stew, braise, boil (roast)
	Cutlets	grill, fry
	Gigot chops	grill, fry
	Head	soup, stock
	Leg	roast, stew, braise
	Loin chops	grill, fry
	Loin and saddle	roast
	Neck – best end	stew, braise
	– middle neck	stew
	Scrag end neck	soup, stock
	Shoulder	roast, stew, braise, boil
Pork	Belly	boil
	Bladebone	roast, boil
	Hand and spring	boil
	Head	boil
	Leg	roast, boil
	Loin	roast, boil
	Loin chops	fry, grill
	Spare rib	roast, boil
	Spare rib chops	fry, grill
	Trotter	stock, soup
Veal	Best end of neck	roast
	Best end of neck chops	grill, fry
	Breast	roast, stew, braise, boil
	Chump end of loin	roast
	Escalopes	grill, fry

	Feet	stock, soup, boil
	Fillet	roast, grill, fry, stew, braise
	Head	boil
	Knuckle	stew, braise, stock, soup
	Loin	roast
	Loin chops	grill, fry
	Middle, scrag end neck	stew, braise
	Shoulder	roast
Bacon	Back and ribs	roast, bake, grill
	End collar	boil, braise
	Flank	boil, braise
	Forehock	boil, braise
	Long back	grill, fry, boil, braise
	Oyster	boil, braise
	Prime collar	grill, fry, boil, braise
	Prime streaky	grill, fry
	Short back	grill, fry
	Thin streaky	grill, fry
	Top streaky, joint	roast, bake
	Top streaky, rashers	grill, fry
Gammon	Corner gammon	grill, fry, boil, braise
	Gammon hock	boil, braise
	Gammon slipper	grill, fry, roast, bake, boil, braise
	Middle gammon	grill, fry, roast, bake, boil, braise

Shepherd's Pie

METRIC/IMPERIAL
1 large onion
2 or 3 tomatoes
25 g/1 oz dripping or lard
350 g/12 oz minced beef
300 ml/½ pint gravy or stock
salt and pepper
generous pinch of mixed herbs
450-675 g/1-1½ lb cooked potatoes
50 g/2 oz butter or margarine
2 tablespoons milk

Serves 4

Peel and slice the onion and tomatoes. Fry in the dripping or lard until tender. Add the meat, gravy or stock, seasoning and mixed herbs. Vary the amount of stock according to personal taste. Simmer gently for 25-30 minutes, stirring well, until the meat is nearly cooked. Place in the bottom of a pie dish.

Mash the potatoes with half the butter or margarine and the milk. When they are very soft and smooth pile on top of the meat mixture. Fork into an attractive shape. Put the remaining butter or margarine in tiny pieces over the potato and bake in the centre of a moderately hot oven (200°C, 400°F, Gas Mark 6) for 30 minutes, until the top is crisp and brown.

Variation

Madras Shepherd's Pie: prepare the meat and vegetable mixture as the recipe above, but stir 1-2 teaspoons curry powder into the meat mixture. Mix 175 g/6 oz grated Cheddar cheese with the mashed potatoes, and cook as the traditional Shepherd's Pie above.

❋ Freezes well for 3 months.

Spiced Baked Gammon

METRIC/IMPERIAL
1 corner piece gammon, about 1.5-1.75 kg/3-4 lb
French mustard
demerara sugar
whole cloves
For the sauce:
4 tablespoons soy sauce
4 tablespoons tarragon vinegar
4 tablespoons pineapple syrup
4 tablespoons tomato ketchup
generous pinch of cayenne pepper
½ teaspoon dry mustard
½ teaspoon garlic salt
2 tablespoons clear honey
To garnish:
pineapple rings
glacé cherries

Serves 6-8

Soak the gammon overnight in cold water. Drain, wrap in foil and bake in a moderately hot oven (190°C, 375°F, Gas Mark 5), allowing 25 minutes per 450 g/per lb and 25 minutes over.

Drain the pineapple rings. Mix all the ingredients for the sauce together and boil for 2-3 minutes.

When the gammon is cooked, remove the foil and strip off the skin. Spread the fat with French mustard and demerara sugar and, using a sharp knife, make cuts in the fat to form diamond shapes. Insert cloves between the diamonds. Return the gammon to the oven, standing it on a rack in the roasting tin. Pour the sauce over and bake for about 15 minutes, basting from time to time with the sauce.

Dip the pineapple rings in the sauce and brown under a heated grill. Serve the gammon garnished with pineapple rings with a glacé cherry in the centre of each. Serve the remaining sauce separately.

❋ Cooked gammon should be frozen for 1 month only.

Lancashire Hot-Pot

METRIC/IMPERIAL
675 g/1½ lb neck of lamb, middle or
best end
salt and pepper
2 large potatoes
2 carrots
1 small turnip
1 large onion or 2 leeks
about 450 ml/¾ pint water
meat dripping or margarine

Serves 4

Season the lamb to taste. Peel and thickly slice the potatoes, carrots, turnip and onion. If using leeks instead of onion, trim, rinse thoroughly under cold running water and cut into 2.5-cm/1-inch pieces.

Place the lamb, potatoes, carrots, turnip and onion in layers in a deep casserole, adding additional salt and pepper to taste. Finish with an overlapping layer of potatoes. Add enough of the water to reach about one-third of the way up the casserole. Place small pats of meat dripping or margarine on top of the potatoes.

Cover the casserole and cook in a cool oven (150°C, 300°F, Gas Mark 2) for 2½-3 hours. Remove the cover about 30 minutes before the end of cooking and increase the temperature to moderately hot (200°C, 400°F, Gas Mark 6) to brown the top layer of potatoes. Lancashire hot-pot is traditionally served with pickled red cabbage.

✳ Freezes well for 3 months.

Braised Topside

METRIC/IMPERIAL
15 g/½ oz flour
salt and pepper
piece of topside beef, about 1.5 kg/3 lb
25 g/1 oz lard or dripping
2 rashers bacon
2 onions
4 carrots
25 g/1 oz butter or dripping
150 ml/¼ pint stock
150 ml/¼ pint red wine
1 bouquet garni

Serves 6

1 Mix the flour, salt and pepper. Coat the beef with the seasoned flour. Brown on either side in the hot lard or dripping in a large pan. Meanwhile chop the bacon and peel and slice the onions and carrots. Lift the meat out of the pan, heat the butter or dripping and fry the chopped bacon and sliced vegetables for 5-6 minutes.

2 Add the stock, wine, bouquet garni and seasoning. Put the meat back into the pan, lower the heat and cover the pan. Make sure the lid fits tightly so the small quantity of liquid will not evaporate. Simmer gently for 1½ hours. Check once or twice that the mixture (called a mirepoix) is not burning. Add extra stock if necessary.

3 **To serve:** lift the meat out of the pan; slice or carve as usual. Sieve or liquidise the vegetables and liquid to form a thick sauce. Garnish the meat with the bacon and some of the sauce.

NOTE   A piece of beef cooked this way shrinks relatively little. Other vegetables (celery, tomatoes, etc.) may be added to the mirepoix.

❋ Freeze mirepoix and cooked meat separately. Use within 2 months.

Braising
Cuts suitable for braising: for all meat cuts, see *Know Your Cuts*, page 56.

Offal:	Hearts	**Poultry:**	Chicken	**Game:**	Grouse
	Kidneys		Guinea fowl		Hare
	Ox liver				Pigeon
	Oxtail				Ptarmigan
	Sweetbreads				Rabbit
					Squab

Escalopes of Veal

METRIC/IMPERIAL
4 veal escalopes
2-3 tablespoons flour
salt and pepper
1 egg
crisp breadcrumbs
50-75 g/2-3 oz fat or butter
To garnish:
wedges of lemon
sprigs of parsley

Serves 4

Beat the escalopes gently with a rolling pin until very thin. Coat with flour, seasoned with salt and pepper, then dip into beaten egg and cover with crumbs. Fry steadily in shallow fat or butter (or butter and oil mixed) until golden brown on both sides.

Garnish with wedges of lemon and sprigs of parsley, or for a more elaborate garnish, top rings of lemon with freshly chopped hard-boiled egg and parsley, or egg and capers. Excellent with a green salad.

✳ Freeze coated veal for 3-4 months.

Fried Steak and Onions

Choose same quality and cuts of steak as for grilling. Heat a good knob of butter or a tablespoon of oil in the pan and put in the steak. Fry quickly on either side to seal in the flavour. Lower the heat and cook gently for about 10-12 minutes for well-done steak, about 6-8 minutes for medium, and 3-4 minutes for rare, turning once. French or English mustard are the usual accompaniments. Some people like Worcestershire sauce. Tomatoes, mushrooms and watercress are the best garnish, or fried onion rings.

To fry onions: peel and cut onions into rings. Separate the rings, dip in milk and seasoned flour. Shake off surplus flour and fry in shallow or deep fat.

Liver with Orange Slices

METRIC/IMPERIAL
350 g/12 oz calf's or lamb's liver
seasoned flour (flour with salt, pepper,
pinch of mustard, cayenne added)
1 onion
2 cloves garlic
50 g/2 oz butter or margarine
1 tablespoon chopped parsley
pinch of salt
4 tablespoons stock
2 tablespoons red wine or about
1 tablespoon vinegar
2 oranges
little oil
brown sugar

Slice the liver thinly and dip in the seasoned flour. Peel and finely chop the onion and garlic. Melt half the butter or margarine in a frying pan and sauté the liver quickly on both sides until cooked. Remove to the hot serving dish.

Add the remaining butter or margarine to the pan and fry the onion and garlic until soft. Add the parsley, pinch of salt, stock and wine or vinegar. Bring to the boil and pour over the liver.

Cut the oranges into thin slices, brush with oil, sprinkle with brown sugar and brown quickly under the grill. Serve immediately with cauliflower and potatoes.

Hamburgers

METRIC/IMPERIAL
1 large or 2 medium onions, grated
450 g/1 lb minced beef
salt and pepper
½ teaspoon dried mixed herbs
1 heaped teaspoon chopped parsley
1 teaspoon Worcestershire sauce
1 large potato

Serves 4

1 Peel and grate the onions. Put the meat into a basin and add the grated onion, seasoning, herbs, parsley and Worcestershire sauce. Lastly, peel and grate in the potato. Mix thoroughly. There will be no need to add liquid as the potato binds the mixture together.

2 Form into 4 large flat cakes and either fry steadily in hot fat or bake on a well-greased tin in a moderately hot oven (200°C, 400°F, Gas Mark 6) for about 25-30 minutes. If liked, the cakes can be floured or tossed in crisp breadcrumbs before cooking. Serve hot and if wished, with a fried egg on top, or for more colourful garnishes, serve on hot toasted bread or buns with rings of raw apple, onion, chopped chives or spring onions, cucumber, cheese (browned under a grill if wished), yogurt or cherries.

To make cheeseburgers

1 Prepare the hamburger mixture, divide into equal portions and form into 4 flat cakes. Cream 25 g/1 oz butter or margarine with 1 teaspoon made mustard and a pinch each of salt and cayenne. Add 175 g/6 oz grated Cheddar cheese and 2 tablespoons milk and mix well. Grill or fry the hamburgers for 5 minutes on each side. Spread a generous helping of the cheese mixture over both sides of each.

2 Split 4 hamburger buns and grill to a golden brown. Put a cooked cheeseburger in each bun and close. Serve hot with mustard or ketchup and pickled onions.

 ✳ Prepare and open freeze hamburgers *before* cooking. Separate each hamburger with waxed or greaseproof paper before wrapping. Use within 3 months. (Omit potato when freezing.)

Pork and Bacon Croquettes

METRIC/IMPERIAL
175 g/6 oz minced belly of pork
175 g/6 oz minced streaky or collar bacon
100 g/4 oz fresh white breadcrumbs
1 teaspoon thyme
salt and pepper
2 eggs
fresh white breadcrumbs to coat
little milk
oil or fat for deep frying

Serves 4

Mix the pork, bacon, breadcrumbs, thyme, salt and pepper well together and bind with one of the eggs, beaten. Roll into croquettes and dip in the other egg, beaten with a little milk. Roll in fresh white breadcrumbs. Heat the oil or fat to 180°C/350°F (see page 45) and deep fry the croquettes until golden.

❅ Fry, drain and cool. Open freeze then wrap. Use within 2 months.

Deep-fried Chicken

METRIC/IMPERIAL
4 chicken joints
egg and breadcrumbs or batter for coating
(see page 41)
oil or fat for deep frying

Serves 4

The chicken joints can be coated with egg and crisp breadcrumbs or batter (see page

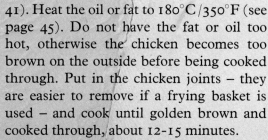

41). Heat the oil or fat to 180°C/350°F (see page 45). Do not have the fat or oil too hot, otherwise the chicken becomes too brown on the outside before being cooked through. Put in the chicken joints – they are easier to remove if a frying basket is used – and cook until golden brown and cooked through, about 12-15 minutes.

Drain on crumpled kitchen paper. Serve with a green salad.

✳ Coated, uncooked chicken can be frozen for 5 months, cooked chicken for up to 3 months. Open freeze then wrap. Batter-coated chicken is not suitable for home freezing.

Scotch Eggs

METRIC/IMPERIAL
4 eggs, hard-boiled
350-450 g/12 oz-1 lb sausagemeat
1 tablespoon flour
salt and pepper
1 egg
50 g/2 oz crisp breadcrumbs
oil or fat for deep frying
To garnish:
watercress
wedges of tomato

Serves 4

Shell the hard-boiled eggs. Divide the sausagemeat into four and pat out into rounds on a floured board. Wrap the eggs in the sausagemeat, making sure this is completely sealed without any air space or cracks. Brush with beaten egg. Roll in breadcrumbs (see page 41 for coating in egg and breadcrumbs). Heat the oil or fat to 180°C/350°F (see page 45). Put in the Scotch eggs. Fry steadily for about 5-8 minutes until crisp and golden brown. Lift out, drain on crumpled kitchen paper and serve hot or cold, garnished with watercress and wedges of tomato.

✳ Do not freeze any dishes containing hard-boiled eggs.

Mixed Grill

A mixed grill can be made from a variety of ingredients, but your grill is made or marred by the way it is served. Have the various grills attractively arranged on the plate, with a suitable garnish to add colour and variety. Watercress is the most usual garnish for a mixed grill, particularly if it includes steak, but try also potato crisps, cucumber slices, green peas, uncooked quartered tomatoes or thinly sliced red pepper. For the grill itself, choose from the following:

4 lamb chops
4 sausages
4 small portions liver
4 lamb's or calf's kidneys
2-4 rashers bacon
tomatoes
mushrooms
butter for basting

There is no reason why veal or pork chops, or cutlets, could not be used instead of lamb, but a lamb chop is the most general choice. The secret of a good mixed grill is to time the cooking carefully; start with food that takes the longest cooking, then gradually add the other ingredients. Do make sure the grill is really hot before cooking and keep kidneys, steak and liver well basted with butter. Remember kidneys are easily over-cooked, so add these towards the end. Sausages on the other hand require a fair amount of cooking.

With most grills, tomatoes and mushrooms can be cooked in the grill pan, while the meats are cooked on the grid. It is advisable to put the pan with the mushrooms and tomatoes underneath for a few minutes to give them a start, before covering with the grid and meat. Serve with vegetables, or a crisp green salad.

Grilled Ham with Corn Fritters

METRIC/IMPERIAL
4 slices gammon
25 g/1 oz butter
For the fritters:
100 g/4 oz self-raising flour
pinch of salt
1 egg
175 ml/6 fl oz milk
1 (198-g/7-oz) can sweet corn
fat for frying
watercress to garnish

Serves 4

Do not preheat the grill when cooking bacon or ham. Snip the edges of the gammon, brush the lean with melted butter and place under the grill. Cook steadily until the fat is golden brown and the meat tender.

Meanwhile sift the flour with the salt, add the egg, milk and drained sweet corn. Fry spoonfuls of this in deep hot fat until crisp and golden brown on both sides. Drain on crumpled kitchen paper and keep hot.

Serve the gammon with the corn fritters and garnish with watercress.

Grilled Chicken

METRIC/IMPERIAL
1 frying chicken, about 1 kg/2 lb
1 lemon
salt
about 50 g/2 oz butter, melted
1 tablespoon sugar
$\frac{1}{4}$ teaspoon paprika
To garnish:
watercress
potato crisps

Serves 4

Using a strong cook's knife, split the chicken in half lengthways by cutting along the breastbone and down through the backbone. Rub the cut lemon, squeezing a little to release the juice, all over the chicken and sprinkle with salt. Brush both sides with melted butter.

Place cut side uppermost in the bottom of the grill pan (grid removed) and cook under medium to low heat for 8-10 minutes. Turn skin-side uppermost and sprinkle evenly with mixed sugar and paprika. Continue grilling for a further 10-15 minutes, or until cooked, brushing frequently with melted butter.

This rich chicken needs no other garnish than a bunch of watercress and potato crisps. To serve, divide each half in half again, cutting between the wing and thigh. Serve with caper sauce.

Caper sauce
Make a white sauce (see page 84) using 150 ml/$\frac{1}{4}$ pint milk and 150 ml/$\frac{1}{4}$ pint chicken stock. Add a little of the caper vinegar to the stock and 2 teaspoons capers to the finished sauce.

To Roast Meat

If you have prime fresh meat (tender meat that has been well-hung), undoubtedly, in my opinion, the best method of cooking is by Method A – Quick Roasting. If on the other hand you are cooking chilled meat or defrosted frozen meat the texture and tenderness will be better by Method B – Slower Roasting.

Most joints are better defrosted before cooking but they can be cooked by Method B if you have not defrosted the meat first. (The exception is whole poultry which *must* be defrosted before roasting.) You need to allow approximately 50% longer cooking time, i.e. a joint that takes 2 hours if fresh or defrosted would take approximately 3 hours if cooking from frozen. You note I have used the word 'approximately' for it is difficult to judge the timing exactly, unless you invest in a meat thermometer which registers the state of the cooked meat.

Personally, beef is really the only meat I find acceptable by this method.

Ovens vary slightly so you must judge which of the two settings is better. You can do this by checking on the degree of doneness of the meat.

Quick Roasting – Method A
Set the oven to 200-220°C, 400-425°F, Gas Mark 6-7. With larger joints you can re-set to 190°C, 375°F, Gas Mark 5 after about 1 hour if the meat is cooking too rapidly.

Slower Roasting – Method B
Set the oven to 160-180°C, 325-350°F, Gas Mark 3-4. Keep at this temperature all the time.

If wrapping in foil or using a covered roasting tin, allow an extra 10-15 minutes at Method A or 20 minutes at Method B.

If using roaster bags do not increase the cooking time.

Quantities of meat to allow
225-350 g/8-12 oz per person (with bone)
175-225 6/6-8 oz per person (without bone).

Always weigh meat or poultry *with* stuffing to ascertain cooking time.

	Roasting Cuts	Time	Accompaniment
Beef	Sirloin, ribs, fillet, rump, aitchbone, topside. *Slow roast:* above cuts and best brisket.	**A:** 15 minutes per 450 g/1 lb plus 15 minutes over (rare). 20 minutes per 450 g/1 lb plus 20 minutes over (well done). **B:** 25 minutes per 450 g/1 lb plus 25 minutes over (rare). 30-35 minutes per 450 g/1lb plus 30-35 minutes over (medium to well done).	*Serve with* gravy, horseradish cream, Yorkshire pudding, mustard.
Lamb–for Mutton use **B** only.	Breast of lamb, best end of neck (lamb), shoulder, leg, saddle. *Slow roast:* above cuts and mutton.	**A:** 20 minutes per 450 g/1 lb plus 20 minutes over. **B:** 35 minutes per 450 g/1 lb plus 35 minutes over.	*Serve lamb with* gravy, mint sauce, mint jelly. *Serve mutton with* gravy, onion sauce, redcurrant jelly.
Pork	Loin, leg, bladebone, spare ribs.	**A:** 25 minutes per 450 g/1 lb plus 25 minutes over. **B:** 40 minutes per 450 g/1 lb plus 40 minutes over. For crisp crackling, score the skin and brush with oil before cooking.	*Serve with* gravy, sage and onion stuffing, apple sauce, mustard.

Veal	Shoulder, breast, best end of neck, loin, fillet, chump end of loin, leg.	**A:** 25 minutes per 450 g/1 lb plus 25 minutes over. **B:** 40 minutes per 450 g/1 lb plus 40 minutes over. Keep well basted with fat.	*Serve with* gravy, sausages, various stuffings.
Bacon	Gammon slipper, middle gammon, back, ribs; streaky joint. Soak overnight in cold water if salted.	**A:** 20 minutes per 450 g/1 lb plus 20 minutes over. **B:** 35 minutes per 450 g/1 lb plus 35 minutes over.	*Serve with* gravy, Cumberland sauce, apple sauce, redcurrant jelly.
Rabbit	Whole animal. Wash rabbit in vinegared water to whiten flesh. Baste with extra fat. Stuff to prevent drying.	**A:** Roast for about 1½ hours at 200°C, 400°F, Gas Mark 6.	*Serve with* sausagemeat or sage and onion stuffing, onion sauce.
Chicken	Good roasting fowl or capon. Frozen birds should be thoroughly defrosted at room temperature. Allow 1.25-1.5 kg/2½-3 lb for 4.	**A:** 15 minutes per 450 g/1 lb plus 15 minutes over. **B:** 25 minutes per 450 kg/1 lb plus 25 minutes over.	*Serve with* gravy, bread sauce, sausages, bacon rolls.
Turkey	Whole stuffed bird. (If starting at 220°C, 425°F, Gas Mark 7 reduce to 200°C, 400°F, Gas Mark 6 after about 1 hour.) Allow up to 350 g/12 oz per person.	**A:** For birds up to 5.5 kg/12 lb, 15 minutes per 450 g/1 lb and 15 minutes over. For every 450 g/1 lb over 5.5 kg/12 lb, allow an extra 12 minutes. **B:** For birds up to 5.5 kg/12 lb, 25 minutes per 450 g/1 lb and 25 minutes over. For every 450 g/1 lb over 5.5 kg/12 lb, allow an extra 20 minutes.	*Serve with* gravy, bread sauce, sausages, cranberry sauce, various stuffings.
Duck or Goose	Whole stuffed bird. Prick the skin gently every 30 minutes for excess fat to run out. Allow small duckling for 2 people. 350-450 g/12 oz-1 lb goose per person (bones weigh heavily in goose.)	**Duck:** See timing for chicken. **Goose:** See timing for turkey.	*Serve with* gravy, sage and onion stuffing, apple sauce, bigarade sauce.
Pigeon	Whole stuffed bird. Really old birds should be casseroled.	Young birds 35-40 minutes at **A**. Older birds 1¼ hours at **B**.	*Serve with* game chips, fried crumbs.
Pheasant or Grouse	Whole bird can be stuffed if desired. Really old birds should be casseroled.	Young birds 1 hour at **A**. Older birds about 1¾ hours at **B**.	*Serve with* redcurrant jelly, bread sauce, game chips, fried crumbs, watercress.

Sage and Onion Stuffing

METRIC/IMPERIAL
2 large onions
300 ml/½ pint water
25 g/1 oz suet or butter
generous pinch each salt and pepper
50 g/2 oz fresh breadcrumbs
1 teaspoon dried sage or 2-3 teaspoons
chopped fresh sage
1 egg

Serves 4

Peel the onions and put into a saucepan with the water. Simmer steadily for about 20 minutes then remove on to a chopping board and chop into small pieces. Transfer to a basin then add all the other ingredients. Add a little onion stock if wished. This is sufficient for a duck. For a large goose use about 3 times the quantity.

✳ Can be frozen for 3 months.

Bread Sauce

METRIC/IMPERIAL
1 small onion
3 cloves (optional)
300 ml/½ pint milk
50 g/2 oz fresh breadcrumbs
salt and pepper
25 g/1 oz butter

Serves 4

Peel the onion and stick the cloves, if used, into it. Put in a pan with the milk and remaining ingredients. Bring the milk slowly to the boil, remove from the heat and leave in a warm place. Before serving, gently heat the sauce, stirring with a wooden spoon. Remove the onion.

✳ Can be frozen for 3 months.

Gravy

Leave the residue from the roast meat in the tin, together with 1 tablespoon fat. Stir in 15 g/½ oz flour, or flour and a little gravy browning. Gradually blend in 450 ml/¾ pint stock (this can be from cooked vegetables), bring to the boil and cook until clear and slightly thickened. Strain and serve. If a thicker gravy is desired, double the quantity of flour used. *Serves 4.*

Cumberland Sauce

METRIC/IMPERIAL
1 teaspoon arrowroot or cornflour
3 tablespoons water
juice of 1 large orange
juice of 1 lemon
salt and pepper
1-2 teaspoons made mustard
3 tablespoons port wine
6 tablespoons redcurrant jelly

Serves 4

Blend the arrowroot or cornflour with the water in a pan. Add the fruit juices and seasoning and stir in the remaining ingredients. Bring slowly to the boil and simmer until the jelly is dissolved. Serve hot or cold with bacon or ham.

✳ This sauce freezes well for 4 months.

Game Chips

Peel potatoes and cut into wafer-thin slices. Dry well and cook in deep fat until crisp and golden brown. Drain well.

Mint Sauce

Measure about 150 ml/¼ pint mint leaves, loosely packed. Finely chop the mint with a little sugar on the board to retain the flavour. Put into a container. Add 3-4 tablespoons vinegar and 1 tablespoon sugar. If a little boiling water is added to the chopped mint before adding the vinegar, the sugar will dissolve more readily. Alternatively, all the ingredients can be put into a liquidiser. *Serves 4-6*.

※ The complete sauce can be frozen for 4 months, the chopped mint – with or without sugar – for 6 months.

Yorkshire Pudding

METRIC/IMPERIAL
100 g/4 oz plain flour
generous pinch of salt
1 egg
300 ml/½ pint milk (or half milk, half water)
knob of lard or dripping

Serves 4

Sift the flour and salt together into a basin, drop in the egg, then beat the mixture well. Gradually beat in just enough liquid to make a stiff batter. Beat until smooth, leave for about 5 minutes, then gradually beat in the rest of the liquid. A batter like this can be left for some time before being cooked. Keep it in the coolest place possible.

When ready to cook, put a knob of lard or dripping into a Yorkshire pudding tin (measuring 10 × 13 cm/7 × 5 inches) and heat in a hot oven (220°C, 425°F, Gas Mark 7) for a few minutes. Pour in the batter and cook for about 30 minutes. In every type of cooker use the top of the oven which is the hottest position. To save cooking time you can cook the batter in small patty tins. Put a piece of fat (the size of a large pea) in each tin, heat this, then pour in the batter and cook for about 15-20 minutes at the top of a hot oven.

Another way of cooking Yorkshire pudding is in the meat tin. Pour away most of the fat, pour in the batter, then stand the meat on a trivet over the meat tin so the juice from the meat continues to drip into the tin, flavouring the pudding. This method of cooking gives a flatter pudding. Serve as soon as cooked with roast beef.

Osso Buco

METRIC/IMPERIAL
3 onions
3 carrots
3 tomatoes
1 stick celery
675 g-1 kg/1½-2 lb knuckle of veal
25 g/1 oz flour
salt and pepper
25 g/1 oz butter or 1 tablespoon oil
1 bouquet garni
grated rind and juice of 1 lemon
300 ml/½ pint white wine or chicken stock
1 tablespoon tomato purée
300 ml/½ pint water
dash of Tabasco sauce (optional)
chopped parsley to garnish

Serves 4

Peel and slice the onions, carrots and tomatoes, and chop the celery. Cut the meat into fairly large, neat pieces. Roll in flour, seasoned with salt and pepper. Fry the onions in hot butter or oil until pale golden. Add the meat, carrots, celery, tomatoes, bouquet garni and seasoning. Toss with the onions for 2-3 minutes. Stir in the lemon rind and juice, white wine or stock, tomato purée diluted with the water and a dash of Tabasco sauce. Cover and simmer for 2 hours. Lift the meat on to a hot dish. Remove the bouquet garni and rub the sauce through a sieve. Pour over the meat and top with chopped parsley. Serve with cooked rice.

❋ Although osso buco can be frozen for 2-3 months, the veal loses its deliciously sticky texture.

Rich Rabbit Stew

METRIC/IMPERIAL
1 rabbit, with liver
100 g/4 oz streaky bacon
18 button onions
50 g/2 oz butter
40 g/1½ oz flour
600 ml/1 pint hot stock
1 bouquet garni
2-3 cloves
6 peppercorns
salt and pepper
150 ml/¼ pint red wine (optional)

Serves 4

Joint the rabbit, dice the bacon and peel the onions. Brown the onions and bacon in the butter and set aside. Then fry the rabbit joints until lightly browned, add the flour and continue frying until well browned. Replace the onions and bacon, add the hot stock, bouquet garni, cloves, peppercorns and seasoning, cover and simmer gently for 1 hour, or until the rabbit is tender.

About 15 minutes before serving, add the red wine. Chop the rabbit liver and when the sauce again reaches simmering point, add the chopped liver and cook for 10 minutes. Serve at once.

✳ Freezes well for 3 months; add wine when reheating.

Hungarian Goulash

METRIC/IMPERIAL
450 g/1 lb stewing beef
25 g/1 oz dripping
225 g/8 oz onions, thinly sliced
1 clove garlic, crushed (optional)
1 tablespoon paprika
salt and pepper
1 tablespoon plain flour
300-450 ml/½-¾ pint stock or water
3 tablespoons tomato chutney
1 (142-ml/5-fl oz) carton natural yogurt

Serves 4

Cut the meat into 2.5-cm/1-inch cubes and brown quickly in the hot dripping. Remove, and lightly fry the sliced onions and crushed garlic. Add the paprika, seasoning and flour and stir over a low heat. Pour in the stock and bring slowly to the boil, stirring. Return the meat to the pan, add the tomato chutney and simmer gently for 1½-2 hours.

Just before serving, stir in the yogurt and serve the goulash with buttered noodles or mashed potatoes and sauerkraut.

✳ Freeze for 3 months; add yogurt when reheating.

Curried Lamb with Savoury Rice

METRIC/IMPERIAL
450-575 g/1-1¼ lb lamb, preferably from
the leg
25 g/1 oz flour
salt and pepper
2-4 teaspoons curry powder
1 onion
1 apple
½ lemon
40 g/1½ oz dripping or butter
1 tablespoon chutney
pinch of sugar
about 450 ml/¾ pint hot stock
25 g/1 oz sultanas
For the savoury rice:
175 g/6 oz long-grain rice
1 small onion
15 g/½ oz butter
1-2 tablespoons chopped red and green
peppers

Serves 4

Cut up the lamb into neat pieces and dust
with flour seasoned with salt, pepper and
curry powder.

Peel and slice or chop the onion and
apple, sprinkling the latter with lemon
juice. Fry the onion and meat in the
dripping or butter until the meat is seared.
Stir in the chutney, sugar and a squeeze of
lemon juice. Add the stock gradually,
stirring until the contents of the pan are
well mixed. Cover the pan and lower the
heat. Simmer for 10 minutes. Add the
chopped apple, sultanas and any remaining
lemon juice. Cover the pan again and continue simmering or transfer to a casserole in
a moderate oven (160°C, 325°F, Gas Mark
3). Cook for 1½ hours.

To make savoury rice: cook washed rice
in salted boiling water containing the
onion until tender, 12-15 minutes. Drain
well. Rinse the rice, then reheat on a dish in
a cool oven. Before serving, stir in the
butter and some of the chopped raw

peppers. Make a border of rice in which to
serve the curry. Sprinkle with the remaining chopped peppers.

Serve the curry with side dishes such as
tomato and onion slices and a sweet chutney such as mango.

❋ Freeze curry for 3 months. Cooked
rice freezes for 4-5 months: lightly freeze,
fork to separate the grains then continue
freezing.

Casserole of Liver and Apples

METRIC/IMPERIAL
450 g/1 lb lamb's liver
25 g/1 oz flour
salt and pepper
1 teaspoon dry mustard
2 medium apples, sliced
2 medium onions, sliced
50 g/2 oz fat
6 rashers streaky bacon
300 ml/½ pint water

Serves 4

Cut the liver into thin slices and coat the slices with flour seasoned with salt, pepper and mustard. Peel and slice the apples and onion. Brown the liver lightly in heated fat.

Fill a greased casserole dish with alternate layers of liver, sliced apples and onions, then top with the bacon rashers. Add the water, cover the casserole and cook in a moderate oven (180°C, 350°F, Gas Mark 4) for 1½ hours, removing the lid for the last 20 minutes. Serve with creamy mashed potatoes and spinach.

Creamed Tripe and Onions

METRIC/IMPERIAL
675 g/1½ lb tripe
2 large onions
300 ml/½ pint water
300 ml/½ pint milk
salt and pepper
25 g/1 oz flour
25 g/1 oz butter
To garnish:
paprika
chopped parsley

Serves 4

Cut the tripe into neat pieces. Put into a pan of cold water, bring to the boil and throw away the water. This is known as blanching and has the effect of improving the colour of the tripe.

Peel and thinly slice the onions and put with the tripe, water, half the milk and seasoning into the rinsed saucepan and simmer gently until tender, about 1 hour.

Blend the flour with the remaining milk, add to the tripe, bring to the boil and cook until smooth. Add the butter and a little extra seasoning if required. Serve sprinkled with paprika and chopped parsley.

Boiled Silverside or Brisket of Beef

1 kg/2 lb silverside or brisket, salted or unsalted
1 large onion
4-5 cloves
2 carrots
1 bay leaf
sprig of parsley
1 medium onion
little butter
25 g/1 oz flour
To garnish:
1 large apple
butter for frying

Serves 4-6

If your joint of beef is salted, soak for several hours in cold water, place in fresh cold water, bring to the boil gently and allow to simmer for 1 hour. Change the water. If the beef is unsalted, simply cover the meat with cold water. Peel the large onion and stud with the cloves. Peel and quarter the carrots and add to the meat with the onion, bay leaf and parsley. Bring to the boil and cook gently, allowing 20 minutes per 450 g/per lb and 20 minutes over.

Meanwhile peel and chop the remaining onion, heat the butter in a small pan, and cook the onion until golden brown. Sprinkle in the flour, stir well and cook for a few minutes. Gradually add 300 ml/½ pint boiling stock from the beef, stirring all the time. Cook gently for 20 minutes, stirring from time to time.

When cooked, slice the meat, cover with the onion sauce and garnish with apple slices fried in butter.

❅ Freeze the cooked meat for up to 6 weeks only.

Steak and Kidney Pudding

For the suet crust pastry:
225 g/8 oz self-raising flour or plain flour with 2 teaspoons baking powder
pinch of salt
110 g/4 oz finely shredded suet
about 150 ml/¼ pint water
For the filling:
450 g/1 lb stewing steak
100 g/4 oz ox kidney
2 tablespoons flour
salt and pepper
2 tablespoons stock or water

Serves 4

Sift the flour, baking powder if used and salt into a bowl. Add the suet. Using a round-bladed knife, mix in enough water to form a light elastic dough.

Turn the pastry on to a lightly floured board. Set aside one-third for the lid and roll out the remainder thinly to a circle

5 cm/2 inches wider than the top of a 1-litre/1½ pint pudding basin. Sprinkle with flour lightly, fold the pastry in half, then in half again to form a triangle. Grease the pudding basin well and insert the pastry, pointed end downwards. Unfold carefully to line the basin.

Cut the steak and kidney into small pieces and roll in the flour, seasoned with salt and pepper. Put into the basin and add the stock or water.

Roll out the remaining pastry to form a lid, cover the pudding and seal the edges with cold water. Cover with greased paper or aluminium foil, steam rapidly for 1½ hours then steadily for 2-2½ hours.

✻ Freeze in its prepared state or cooked. Use within 3 months. The pudding should be under-cooked to prevent the meat becoming over-cooked when reheated.

Chicken Supreme

METRIC/IMPERIAL
1 carrot
1 onion
1 boiling or roasting chicken
1 bouquet garni
1-2 teaspoons salt

For the sauce:
50 g/2 oz butter or margarine
50 g/2 oz flour
300 ml/½ pint chicken stock (see method)
300 ml/½ pint milk
salt and pepper
2 egg yolks
4 tablespoons single cream
parsley to garnish

Serves 4-6

Peel and halve the carrot and onion. Place the chicken in a large pan with the prepared vegetables, bouquet garni, salt and sufficient water to cover. Bring the water to the boil, remove any scum and reduce the heat. Cover with a lid and simmer for 2-3 hours until tender. If using roasting chicken allow 20 minutes per 450 g/per lb.

Slice or joint the boiled chicken and keep hot in a little of the chicken stock. Strain 300 ml/½ pint stock from the liquid. Heat the butter or margarine, then stir in the flour and cook for several minutes. Gradually blend in the chicken stock and milk. Add seasoning, bring to the boil and cook until the sauce is smooth and thick. Remove from the heat.

Blend the egg yolks and cream and strain into the hot sauce. Cook for several minutes without boiling. Either coat the chicken with the sauce or serve separately. If coating the chicken, lift the meat from the stock and drain well. If serving separately, the chicken may be served in a very little stock if wished. Garnish with sprigs of parsley or chopped parsley.

✻ Can be frozen for 3 months.

To Carve Meat

Beef

Carve large thin slices *across* the joint. Where sirloin of beef is cooked on the bone you should first remove the backbone or chine, then cut the first slices along the bone. Next turn the joint and cut slices at right angles from the bone.

Lamb or mutton

Cut thickish slices *downwards*, but with certain joints it is best to carve in the following way:

Saddle

Cut very long slices first across the centre of the joint, cutting these downwards. Next cut slices from either end of the saddle, finally cut rather slanting from the remainder of the joint.

Shoulder

Turn the joint with the thickest part uppermost. Cut a long thick slice from the centre of the joint down to the bone. Carve thick slices from both sides. Follow the contour of the bone and cut slices round this. If the end of the shoulder bone is held in a napkin it gives one a firmer hold. Turn the joint over and carve thin horizontal slices from the remaining meat.

Pork

Cut shoulder of pork like lamb, and also the leg. Loin of pork should be easy to cut since the skin is scored before cooking to give a good crackling and the butcher generally saws through the bones. Cut slices downwards.

Veal

The method of carving depends on the joint. Legs or shoulder are carved downwards or round the bone like lamb, loin is cut downwards into chops, fillet is carved across as beef.

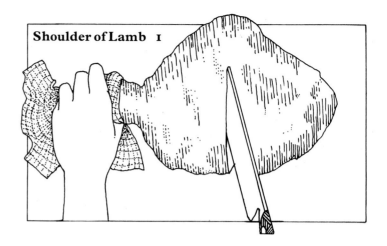

Shoulder of Lamb 1

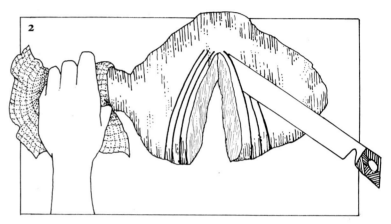

2

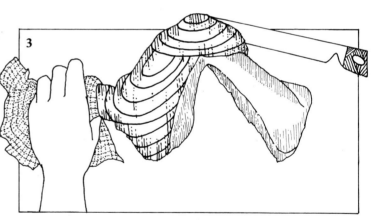

3

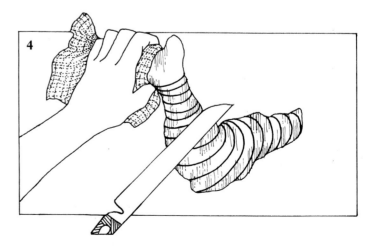

4

To Carve Poultry

Chicken
The method of carving depends on the size of the bird.

For very tiny spring chickens serve one per person, or, if slightly larger, cut into halves – if you cut firmly down, slightly to one side of the centre of the breast bone, it is quite easy to do.

Medium chickens can be jointed, rather than carved, making one or two joints of each of the legs and two joints of the breast and wings. A large chicken is carved like a turkey.

Turkey and Goose
Either cut off the leg on one side or pull it well away from the body. This enables you to cut really large slices from the breast.

When sufficient meat from the breast has been cut, carve the meat from the leg.

Duck
Small ducklings can be cut into halves, like tiny chickens, for there is not a lot of meat on the breast. Cut the large birds into four joints – 2 from the breast and 2 from the legs. For a very large duck, rather thick slices can be cut from the breast instead of serving the breast uncut.

Game
Small birds are served whole or halved – larger birds carved or jointed like chicken. Venison is carved like lamb.

The heat of the joint quickly blunts a carving knife – so if you are carving for a lot of people it is wise to use two knives alternately.

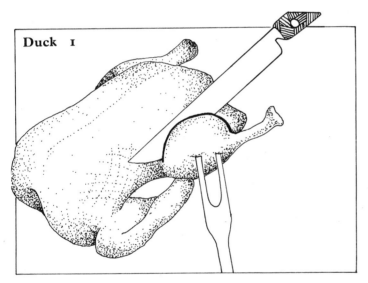

Duck 1

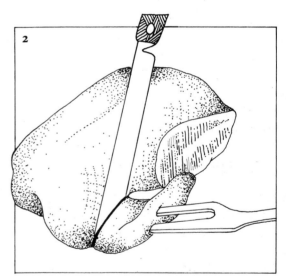

2

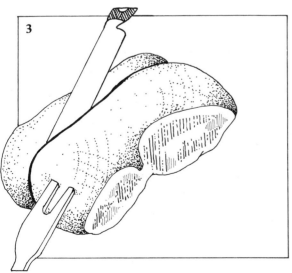

3

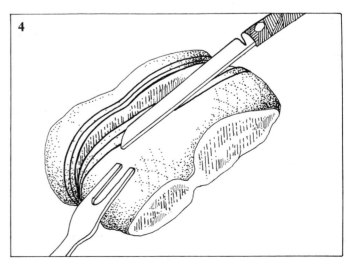

4

Sauces

Secrets of Success

There are a number of points to consider when cooking sauces.

Firstly, your choice. This should complement the main ingredients with which it is to be served, adding flavour but never overwhelming the basic foods.

Secondly, allow yourself adequate time to prepare and cook the sauce. If you try to rush the process, the sauce could be inadequately cooked and have a poor taste and texture.

Select your equipment carefully for sauce-making. You need a good-sized saucepan, which will allow adequate space for stirring or whisking. Have a good strong wooden spoon to stir the ingredients, plus a balloon whisk.

Always check the sauce as it cooks; taste it critically and add flavouring and seasonings gradually.

In most sauces the liquid should be brought to boiling point, then the heat reduced, so the sauce simmers until cooked. During these stages, stirring or whisking is essential to ensure a smooth sauce. If, in spite of your efforts, the sauce does develop small lumps, then you could put the sauce into a liquidiser for a short time. Pour the sauce back into the saucepan and allow it to simmer steadily until thickened.

A number of sauces, such as Hollandaise, page 87, are based on egg yolks. It is essential that these are cooked over hot, but not boiling, water and whisked briskly during cooking. Egg-based sauces will curdle if cooked over too great a heat.

Some sauces can be successfully frozen and information about freezing is given under the recipes.

Basic White Sauce

METRIC/IMPERIAL
coating consistency :
25 g/1 oz butter or margarine
25 g/1 oz flour
300 ml/½ pint milk
salt and pepper
panada (binding consistency) :
as above but use 150 ml/¼ pint milk
thin sauce for soups :
as above but use 600 ml/1 pint milk

Roux method: heat the butter or margarine gently, remove from the heat and stir in the flour. Return to the heat and cook gently for a few minutes, so that the 'roux', as the butter and flour mixture is called, does not brown.

Again remove the pan from the heat and gradually blend in the cold milk. Bring to the boil, then cook, stirring with a wooden spoon, until smooth. Season well and serve.

Blending method: mix the flour with a few tablespoons of the milk and blend to a smooth paste. Bring the remaining milk to the boil.

Pour the milk over the flour paste and return the mixture to the pan. Stirring continuously, bring to the boil over a low heat. Simmer for 2-3 minutes until thick. Add the seasoning and cook for 5 minutes.

Variations on white sauce
Cheese sauce: stir in 75 g/3 oz grated cheese when the sauce has thickened, add mustard.
Parsley sauce: add about 1 tablespoon chopped parsley.
Béchamel sauce: infuse a piece each of very finely chopped onion, carrot, celery in milk. Strain and make as white sauce.
Onion sauce: make a white sauce using 150 ml/¼ pint milk and 150 ml/¼ pint onion stock. Add 2 medium onions which have been simmered until soft in salted water and chopped.

Brown Sauce

METRIC/IMPERIAL
25 g/1 oz fat or dripping
25 g/1 oz flour
300 ml/½ pint brown stock
salt and pepper

1 The method of making is the same as for white sauce by the 'roux' method. A sauce with more flavour is made by frying a finely chopped onion and carrot in the fat until lightly brown.

2 Add the flour to the vegetables, stir in and cook until the flour is lightly browned. Gradually add the stock, stirring all the time. If frying vegetables for a brown sauce, use nearly 50 g/2 oz fat and allow 15 minutes cooking time.

3 The sauce should be strained before using. Brown sauce may also be made by the blending method. The quantities are the same as above. Should you wish to add vegetables in this method, then the chopped onion and carrot must be added to the stock. This should be simmered for about 15 minutes, strained, made up to 300 ml/½ pint again and the sauce made as above.

Egg Sauces

Hollandaise Sauce

METRIC/IMPERIAL
2 egg yolks
pinch of cayenne
salt and pepper
1-2 tablespoons lemon juice or white
wine vinegar
100 g/4 oz butter

Serves 2-4, depending on the dish

1 It is best to use a double saucepan or a bowl over a saucepan of hot water for Hollandaise and similar sauces. Put the egg yolks, seasonings and lemon juice or vinegar into the top of the pan. Whisk over hot but not boiling water until the sauce begins to thicken.

2 Add the butter in very small pieces, whisking in each pat and allowing it to melt before adding the next. DO NOT ALLOW TO BOIL as it will curdle. If too thick, add a little single cream. If the finished sauce separates, remove from the heat and beat in 1 tablespoon water.

Variations
Bearnaise sauce: add 2 teaspoons finely chopped cooked shallots, a little chopped parsley and freshly chopped tarragon or tarragon vinegar. Serve with steak.
Mousseline sauce: use only 25 g/1 oz butter to the 2 egg yolks. Add a little single cream and grated nutmeg. Serve with asparagus, broccoli and other vegetables.

Espagnole Sauce

METRIC/IMPERIAL
1 small onion
1 carrot
1 rasher bacon
2 large mushrooms
25 g/1 oz butter
25 g/1 oz flour
300 ml/½ pint brown stock
1 bouquet garni
2 tablespoons tomato purée
salt and pepper
2 tablespoons sherry

Serves 4

Peel and chop the onion and carrot and chop the bacon and mushrooms. Melt the butter in a pan and fry the prepared vegetables and bacon for 5 minutes, stirring well. Then stir in the flour and cook for 5 minutes more. Gradually blend in the cold stock, add the bouquet garni and bring to the boil, stirring continuously. Stir in the tomato purée and simmer for 40 minutes. Remove the bouquet garni. Season well, sieve and reheat with the sherry.

Bigarade (Orange) Sauce

Prepare an Espagnole sauce. Thinly pare the rind of 1 orange, preferably Seville. Cut into thin strips and simmer these in 150 ml/ ¼ pint water for 10 minutes. Reheat the sieved Espagnole sauce with the orange rind, juice of the orange, 1 tablespoon lemon juice and 2 tablespoons port wine or claret.

Sweet Sour Sauce

METRIC/IMPERIAL
2 tablespoons vinegar
1½ tablespoons sugar
1½ teaspoons tomato ketchup or
tomato purée
2 teaspoons cornflour
1½ teaspoons soy sauce
300 ml/½ pint water
salt
2 teaspoons oil
50-75 g/2-3 oz canned pineapple or
50-75 g/2-3 oz mustard pickles
50 g/2 oz onions, spring onions or
pickled onions

Serves 4

Blend the vinegar, sugar, tomato ketchup
or purée, cornflour and soy sauce with the
water. Pour into a saucepan and cook until
thick. Add the salt and oil and continue
cooking for a few minutes. Finely chop the
pineapple or mustard pickles and onions.
Stir into the sauce.

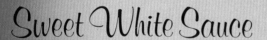

Sweet White Sauce

METRIC/IMPERIAL
1 tablespoon cornflour
300 ml/½ pint milk
25 g/1 oz sugar
15 g/½ oz butter
little vanilla essence

Serves 4

Blend the cornflour with a little cold milk.
Bring the rest of the milk to the boil. Pour
over the cornflour and return to the pan
with the sugar. Bring the sauce to the boil,
stirring all the time. Add the butter and
vanilla essence.

Continue cooking steadily for a few
minutes, stirring well.

Jam Sauce

METRIC/IMPERIAL
4-5 tablespoons jam
juice of 1 lemon
2 tablespoons water

Serves 4

Boil all the ingredients together until the
jam has melted, about 4-5 minutes. Watch
the sauce carefully as it can burn easily.
Sieve the sauce if liked.

Variations
Use marmalade or apple or redcurrant jelly
in place of the jam.
Use a sweetened fruit purée in place of the
jam.

Vegetables and Salads

Secrets of Success

It is important to shop carefully for fresh, good-quality vegetables.

Green vegetables, including lettuce, should look crisp and firm, with no sign of yellow leaves.

Root vegetables should be unblemished, firm and unwrinkled, and tomatoes ripe but firm.

Fresh peas should have firm, full, green pods; if these look even faintly yellow, the peas are either old or stale.

Look for delicious young vegetables – giant beans and marrows may win prizes, but are all too often tough or old and tasteless.

Having selected your vegetables wisely, store them with care. Allow adequate air circulation in a cool dry place. Keep salad ingredients in a covered container in the refrigerator.

The table that follows in this chapter gives various ways of cooking and serving vegetables.

There are various basic techniques in cooking vegetables, the most usual being:

Baking – this retains the full flavour of vegetables.

Boiling – the golden rule is to cook the vegetables in the minimum quantity of boiling salted water for the shortest cooking time to retain their colour, flavour, texture and the maximum vitamin content. Green vegetables should be cooked rapidly, root vegetables need *steady* boiling. Keep the lid on the saucepan during cooking.

Frying – in either shallow or deep fat. It is important that the fat, or oil, is at the right temperature. Drain on absorbent paper.

Grilling – preheat the grill and keep the vegetables well brushed with melted fat.

Roasting – ideal for potatoes, parsnips and onions. Roll the prepared vegetables in the hot dripping or fat to make sure they are evenly coated and cook in a hot oven. Parsnips should be cooked first for 15-20 minutes in boiling salted water.

A golden rule is to cook vegetables as soon as possible after preparation and to serve them as quickly as possible.

Frozen vegetables have been 'blanched' before freezing, i.e. cooked for a very short time in boiling water. Naturally this makes them more tender and the final cooking time should be shortened.

Salad vegetables should be prepared carefully so you have beautifully crisp, fresh-looking salad greens. Enhance the taste of salads with a well-flavoured dressing, as given on page 100.

All About Vegetables

Vegetable	Preparing	Cooking
Artichokes, globe	Trim stem, rinse.	Cook in boiling salted water for about 30 minutes.
Artichokes, Jerusalem	Scrub, peel or scrape. Soak in cold water with a few drops of vinegar.	Cook in boiling salted water with a few drops of vinegar for about 30 minutes.
Asparagus	Wash, trim short piece off white stalk bases.	Steam or boil, tied in bunches in salted water, for 20-25 minutes.
Aubergines	Wash, remove hard stalk. Peel if liked, cut or slice. Salt and stand for 20 minutes.	Use to stuff, casserole (about 20 minutes) or fry until tender on both sides.
Beans, broad	Wash and split young beans, slice. Shell older beans, discarding the pods.	Cook pods separately in boiling salted water for 10 minutes. Cook shelled beans in boiling salted water for about 20 minutes.
French	Top and tail, leave whole.	Cook in boiling salted water for 10-15 minutes.
runner	Trim, remove strings and slice thinly.	Cook in boiling salted water for about 5 minutes.
Beetroot	Wash thoroughly.	Simmer in boiling salted water 30 minutes-2 hours according to size.
Broccoli	Wash and separate spears.	Cook rapidly in boiling salted water for 15-20 minutes.
Brussels sprouts	Wash, remove outer withered leaves. Make a cross in the thick base. Leave whole.	Cook in fast boiling salted water for about 10 minutes.
Cabbage	Wash, shred finely.	Cook in fast boiling salted water for about 10 minutes.
Red cabbage	Wash, shred finely.	Pickle or prepare as cabbage.
Carrots	Scrub, scrape and trim off tops.	Cook in boiling salted water until tender, 15-35 minutes.
Cauliflower	Wash, cut off thick stalks, break into florets.	Cook in fast boiling salted water for 15 minutes.
Celery	Wash and cut into pieces, discard leaves.	Cook in boiling salted water for 20 minutes, or braise with a little butter.
Chicory	Wash and slice.	Boil in salted water for about 20 minutes.
Corn on the cob	Wash, strip off outer leaves and whiskers.	Boil in water for 20 minutes, add salt towards end of cooking. Boil gently.
Courgettes	Need not be peeled, trim off ends.	Cook with garlic in butter and oil, or boil for 20 minutes.

Serving	Freezing
Serve with melted butter, white, cheese or Hollandaise sauce.	Take off outer leaves, trim tops. Blanch in water and a little lemon juice for 7-10 minutes.
Serve with melted butter, white, cheese or Hollandaise sauce.	Boil for 30 minutes. Freeze in purée form for soups.
Serve as an accompaniment or with melted butter or mousseline sauce.	Wash, trim and tie in bunches. Blanch thin stems for 2 minutes and thick stems for 3-4 minutes.
Serve stuffed as a starter or fried as an accompaniment.	Peel, slice into 2.5-cm/1-inch pieces, blanch for 4-5 minutes. Separate with papers.
Serve with melted butter and chopped parsley.	Pod beans and blanch for 3 minutes.
Serve with melted butter.	Blanch for 3 minutes.
Serve with melted butter.	Blanch for 2 minutes.
Serve hot with Hollandaise or parsley sauce or cold with salads.	Cook completely, peel and cut as wished. Freeze small ones whole.
Serve with melted butter or Hollandaise sauce.	Freeze only the best. Trim and wash in salted water. Blanch for 4 minutes and drain.
Serve as an accompaniment with melted butter or with cheese sauce browned under the grill.	Freeze best young sprouts only. Prepare and blanch for 4 minutes.
Serve at once with melted butter. Shred and serve raw in salads.	Prepare as for cooking or keep in wedges. Blanch 1½-3 minutes. Drain.
As cabbage.	As cabbage.
Serve with melted butter and chopped parsley.	Prepare as to cook. Blanch old carrots – freeze young ones unblanched. Store for 2-3 months only.
Serve with white, cheese or parsley sauce, or garnish with fried bread-crumbs and chopped hard-boiled eggs.	Blanch trimmed florets in salted water. Short freeze.
Serve with white, cheese or parsley sauce. Serve chopped raw in salads.	Clean and cut as desired, blanch 3 minutes.
Serve raw, thinly sliced in salads, or as an accompaniment.	Blanch cleaned chicory in lemon water for 2 minutes.
Serve with melted butter.	Blanch prepared cobs for 5-8 minutes. Cool and dry.
Serve as an accompaniment, or with tomatoes, cooked until tender.	Slice and either blanch or sauté in butter for 3 minutes.

All About Vegetables

Vegetable	Preparing	Cooking
Cucumber	Peel if old. Slice thinly for salads.	Braise like celery, or boil in salted water. Or fry until tender.
Fennel	Clean, as celery.	Cook as celery.
Kale	Clean as cabbage or spinach.	Cook as cabbage or spinach.
Leeks	Trim off roots, split lengthways from centre and wash out earth.	Boil in salted water for about 30 minutes.
Mushrooms	Wash cultivated mushrooms. Peel field varieties. Leave button mushrooms whole.	Fry in butter, grill or cover and bake for 30 minutes. Or stew in milk and thicken liquid after cooking.
Okra	Slice fresh okra after washing.	Braise in butter or cook in boiling salted water for 25 minutes.
Onions	Peel and slice. Slice finely for salads or chop finely.	Boil whole for 30-40 minutes in salted water. Fry sliced onion. Use in stews and casseroles.
Parsnips	Scrub well and peel. Cut into even pieces.	Cook in boiling salted water for 15-35 minutes or parboil and roast around a joint of meat.
Peas	Shell and discard pods.	Cook in boiling salted water.
Peppers	Remove stalk and seeds. Wash and shred. Keep whole for stuffing.	Cook in sauces and casseroles.
Potatoes	Peel or scrub.	Cook in boiling salted water for 10-15 minutes. Fry as chips in deep fat. Steam, roast, bake in jackets.
Shallots	As onions.	As onions, or pickle.
Spinach	Wash leaves several times.	Cook with no water and a little salt until tender, 5-10 minutes. Drain off liquid.
Swedes	Peel off thick skin, cut into even pieces.	Cook in boiling salter water or steam for 10-15 minutes.
Sweet potato	Peel, cut into even pieces.	Roast around meat, or boil in salted water for 20-30 minutes.
Turnips	Peel and cut into pieces.	Use in soups and stews—boil in salted water for 20-30 minutes. Cook small turnips whole.
Vegetable marrow	Peel, remove seeds, cut in pieces or halve for stuffing.	Cook in boiling salted water or steam for 30 minutes. Stuff and bake.

Serving	Freezing
Serve raw in salads or as an unusual accompaniment.	Freeze for cooking only. Slice and sauté for 3 minutes.
Serve with white sauce.	Prepare and blanch for 4 minutes. Use for cooking.
Serve with a little melted butter.	Prepare as for cooking and blanch for 2 minutes.
Serve with white or cheese sauce.	Clean and trim, slice and sauté in butter for 4 minutes.
Serve as an accompaniment to grills, stuff as a starter.	Freeze cleaned button mushrooms unblanched (short freeze). Or sauté whole or sliced for a minute.
Serve boiled okra with melted butter.	Trim and blanch for 4 minutes.
Serve boiled with white sauce or fried as an accompaniment to savoury dishes. Serve raw in salads.	Prepare and cut as desired (leave small ones whole). Blanch whole onions for 3 minutes.
Serve as an accompaniment or mash and make into croquettes.	Trim and prepare. Cut as desired and blanch for 3 minutes.
Serve with mint, melted butter and a little sugar.	Shell peas and blanch for a minute. Open freeze.
Serve in savoury dishes. Stuff whole as a main course.	Prepare as for cooking. Cut as desired. Blanch for 3 minutes.
Stuff baked potatoes, mash and cream boiled potatoes. Serve 'Lyonnaise' or scalloped.	If freezing chips, part fry for 2 minutes. Cook new potatoes until tender.
Serve in casseroles or as a pickle.	—
Serve finely chopped with a little milk and butter.	Blanch prepared spinach in small quantities for about 2 minutes.
Serve as an accompaniment, mashed or in pieces.	Trim, peel and dice. Blanch for 3 minutes.
Serve mashed or whole.	—
Serve mashed with butter. Glaze small whole turnips.	Trim, peel and dice. Blanch for 3 minutes or freeze in purée with butter.
Serve with white or cheese sauce.	—

Stuffed Courgettes

METRIC/IMPERIAL
½ small green pepper
4-6 large courgettes
1 (298-g/10½-oz) can condensed Scotch
broth
salt and pepper
175-225 g/6-8 oz cooked lamb, diced
1 teaspoon Worcestershire sauce
To garnish:
parsley
4 tomatoes, sliced

Serves 4

Put the green pepper into boiling salted water for 2-3 minutes, lift out and drain. Chop and remove seeds. Slice off the tops of the courgettes to give a boat shape and remove the seeds. Mix the Scotch broth with seasoning, meat, chopped green pepper and Worcestershire sauce. Stuff the courgettes with this mixture.

Wrap in foil, place in a roasting tin and bake in a moderately hot oven (190°C, 375°F, Gas Mark 5) for 30 minutes. Serve garnished with parsley and lightly grilled tomato slices.

There are many other ways in which courgettes and marrows can be stuffed.

Thick brown sauce (see page 84) can also be used instead of the Scotch broth.

Variations
Fried onion, tomatoes and cooked rice.
Fried onion, tomatoes, capers and minced left-over cooked meat, blended with a thick sauce.
A vegetarian stuffing of a thick cheese sauce with diced cooked vegetables.

Ratatouille

METRIC/IMPERIAL
2 onions
450 g/1 lb tomatoes
salt
1 medium marrow or 225-350 g/8-12 oz
courgettes
4 small aubergines
1 red or green pepper
little bacon fat or rind from gammon
1-2 cloves garlic
chopped parsley to garnish

Serves 4

1 Peel and chop the onions. Peel the tomatoes then cut them in half, sprinkle with salt and leave upturned to drain.

2 Peel the marrow, remove seeds and cut into large chunks. Courgettes should be sliced but not peeled. Remove the stalks from the washed aubergines, cut in half, scoop out slightly and cut into chunks. Wash, seed and slice the pepper. Crush the garlic with salt. Heat the fat or rind in a strong pan and gently fry the onions and the garlic.

3 Remove the rind, if used, and add the aubergines, marrow, tomatoes and pepper. Season well and simmer slowly, with a well-fitting lid on the pan, until the vegetables are tender. Serve sprinkled with parsley.

Cauliflower Polonaise

Wash the cauliflower thoroughly, cut away the thick stalks and break into florets. Cook in boiling salted water for 15 minutes.

Meanwhile fry some fine breadcrumbs in hot butter until brown. Add 1-2 chopped hard-boiled eggs, and 2-3 teaspoons of chopped parsley. Put this mixture over the cauliflower just before serving. Heat more butter to serve separately.

Vegetable Curry

METRIC/IMPERIAL
50 g/2 oz margarine
1 onion
1 apple
1 tablespoon curry powder
1 tablespoon flour
450 g/1 lb mixed vegetables (onions, celery, carrots)
600 ml/1 pint stock
squeeze of lemon juice
2 teaspoons desiccated coconut
1 tablespoon sultanas
1 teaspoon soft brown sugar
2 teaspoons chutney
salt and pepper
100 g/4 oz mushrooms
cooked long-grain rice (see page 116)

Serves 4

Peel and chop the onion and apple and fry in the margarine until soft. Stir in the curry powder and flour and cook for 3-4 minutes. Peel and chop the mixed vegetables. Add to the onion and apple mixture. Gradually add the stock and bring to the boil. Add the mixed vegetables, lemon juice, coconut, sultanas, brown sugar, chutney and seasoning. Cover and simmer for 35 minutes.

Slice the mushrooms, add to the curry and simmer for a further 15 minutes. Spoon into a serving dish and arrange a border of rice round the edge of the dish.

❊ Freezes well for up to 6 months. Vegetables should be under-cooked.

Vegetable Pie

METRIC/IMPERIAL
450 g/1 lb potatoes
450-575 g/1-1¼ lb mixed root vegetables
100 g/4 oz cheese, grated
For the sauce:
25 g/1 oz butter
25 g/1 oz flour
300 ml/½ pint milk or milk and vegetable stock
salt and pepper

Serves 4

Prepare the potatoes and cook in boiling salted water for 10-20 minutes. Drain and cream them with a little milk and butter.

Peel and cut the vegetables into small pieces. Cook until tender, then drain. Make the white sauce (see page 84) with the butter, flour, milk or milk and vegetable stock, and seasoning.

Mix the diced cooked vegetables with the sauce and most of the grated cheese. Put into a pie dish. Top with the creamed potato and the remaining grated cheese.

Cook in a moderately hot oven (200°C, 400°F, Gas Mark 6) for approximately 15 minutes.

❊ Can be frozen for 3 months but is better freshly made.

Baked Potatoes in their Jackets

Scrub good-sized potatoes, dry and prick lightly; if you want a crisp skin, rub with margarine or butter. Bake in a moderately hot oven (190°C, 375°F, Gas Mark 5) for 1–1½ hours. When cooked, the best flavour is produced if they are cut through the centre and left uncovered for a minute or so. Serve with butter and seasoning.

Potatoes Vichy

Bake potatoes in their jackets, then slice off a piece of each potato lengthwise. Scoop out the potato and mix with cream, chopped chives and salt. Replace in the potato skins and reheat if necessary.

Potatoes and Mushrooms

Bake potatoes in their jackets, then halve and mix the potato with fried chopped mushrooms. Season well and return to potato cases. Top with grated cheese and brown under the grill or in the oven. Serve with tomatoes.

Curried Potatoes

Bake potatoes in their jackets and cut off the tops, serrating these if wished. Scoop out the potato and mash well, adding 25 g/1 oz butter and seasoning. Press into potato cases leaving a nest shape. Dice a small slice of bread and an apple. Melt 25 g/1 oz butter in a pan and stir in a generous pinch of curry powder. Add the diced bread and apple with a few raisins. Pile the hot apple mixture into the potato cases.

French Dressing

METRIC/IMPERIAL
½–1 teaspoon made English or French
mustard
shake of pepper
pinch of salt
pinch of sugar
3–4 tablespoons olive, salad or corn oil
1½–2 tablespoons malt or wine vinegar or
lemon juice

Put the mustard, pepper, salt and sugar on to a saucer or plate and gradually blend in the oil then the vinegar.

Alternatively, put them into a clean jar with a screw top, add the oil and vinegar and shake vigorously.

These are the usual proportions of oil and vinegar, but they may be varied to suit personal taste. Chopped fresh herbs or a crushed clove of garlic may be added to flavour the dressing.

To Prepare Green Salads

Lettuce

Be very careful how you handle lettuces, particularly the forced and imported ones obtainable in winter. Wash and dry very gently and very carefully. Do not squeeze very hard. Remove the outer leaves with your fingers or with a stainless steel knife. Separate the leaves and wash in cold water to which a little salt has been added.

Lift out of the salt water and put either into a salad shaker and shake quite dry, or into a teacloth and pat dry. Kitchen paper can be used instead of the teacloth.

Other green vegetables, endive, etc. are prepared in the same way.

Watercress

Cut off the bottom stalks. Divide into sprigs. Wash as lettuce.

Mustard and Cress

Take off the mustard and cress from the stalks, if you buy one of the containers in which it is growing. If not, then you will buy it in a small bunch. Lift out of this, and wash in a very tiny sieve or colander under running cold water. Remove any of the tiny seeds. Dry in a teacloth or kitchen paper.

Green Salad

METRIC/IMPERIAL
1 lettuce
watercress
¼ cucumber
½ small green pepper
French dressing

The ingredients for a green salad should, as the name suggests, be green ingredients only, so do not add tomatoes, hard-boiled egg, beetroot, etc. Shred the lettuce, sprig the watercress, slice the cucumber and the pepper. Toss together in a bowl with dressing to taste.

Endive, chicory, and mustard and cress may be added if wished.

Mixed Salad

METRIC/IMPERIAL
1 lettuce
watercress
¼ cucumber
½ small green pepper
2 tomatoes
few radishes
few spring onions
2 eggs, hard-boiled
French dressing or mayonnaise

Any salad which contains a variety of ingredients could be called a 'mixed salad', but the accepted form is to mix sliced tomatoes, radishes, onions, and eggs with the ingredients in a green salad. Either toss in a French dressing or serve with mayonnaise.

Potato Mixed Salad

METRIC/IMPERIAL
225-350 g/8-12 oz cooked potatoes
2 tomatoes
225 g/8 oz cooked green beans
black olives
French dressing or mayonnaise

Slice or dice the potatoes and tomatoes, mix with the beans and olives. Top with French dressing or mayonnaise. If preferred, mix the ingredients together and toss in the dressing.

Caesar Salad

METRIC/IMPERIAL
1 large slice bread
25-50 g/1-2 oz butter
½ clove garlic
French dressing (see page 100)
1 lettuce
¼ cucumber
1-2 eggs, hard-boiled
2-3 tomatoes
2 tablespoons grated cheese (optional)
4-8 anchovy fillets

1 Dice the bread and fry in the butter until crisp and brown. Drain.

2 Rub round a salad bowl with the garlic.

3 Add all the ingredients for the French dressing and whisk with a fork.

4 Add the lettuce leaves and toss well to combine.
   Slice the cucumber, egg and tomatoes and arrange in the salad bowl. Sprinkle with the grated cheese, if used, and top with anchovy fillets and bread croûtons.

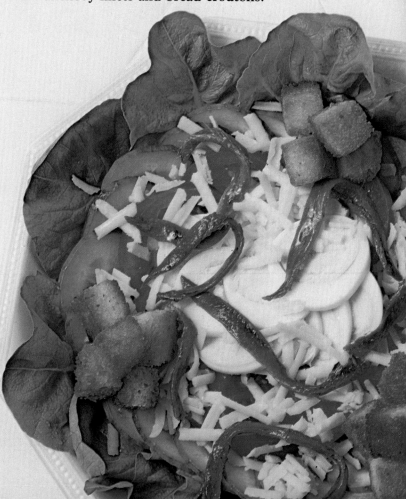

Waldorf Salad

METRIC/IMPERIAL
4 crisp dessert apples
small head celery
75-100 g/3-4 oz walnuts, coarsely chopped
little French dressing
mayonnaise
1 lettuce
lemon juice

Peel and dice the apples, reserving some apple for the garnish. Dice the celery and mix with chopped walnuts and a little French dressing. Just before serving, toss in mayonnaise and pile on to a bed of lettuce. Garnish with apple slices, dipped in a little lemon juice to prevent discoloration, and a halved walnut.

Salad Niçoise

METRIC/IMPERIAL
1 (198-g/7-oz) can tuna fish
3-4 tomatoes
2 eggs, hard-boiled
1 small green pepper
1 (56-g/2-oz) can anchovy fillets
few black olives
few cooked broad beans
French dressing
$\frac{1}{2}$ teaspoon chopped fresh herbs

Drain the oil from the tuna fish (this can be blended with the dressing if wished). Slice the tomatoes and eggs or cut into quarters. Cut the pepper into strips. Mix all the salad ingredients together and toss in the French dressing flavoured with the chopped herbs.

Savoury Dishes

Secrets of Success

This chapter covers the cooking of a variety of foods from which main and light dishes can be prepared: these range from egg and cheese dishes to those made with rice and pasta.

Two golden rules when cooking eggs: never over-cook the food and serve the dish as soon as it is ready. Eggs continue to cook in a hot container, and an over-cooked egg can develop a somewhat unpleasant taste and texture.

Baking – an excellent way of combining eggs with other savoury ingredients, such as cheese, vegetables and cream. They must still be soft when they come from the oven.

Soufflés are also baked. These are surprisingly simple, just a combination of a sauce or purée, flavouring, egg yolks, then stiffly whisked egg whites. Time the baking carefully, so the soufflé can be served as soon as it is cooked.

Boiling – careful timing is an essential feature if the egg is to be cooked perfectly to suit personal tastes. A hard-boiled egg will continue to cook as it cools, which is why you are recommended to crack the shell and plunge the egg into cold water to cool the egg.

Frying – when frying eggs make quite sure the small amount of fat is sufficiently hot to set the egg white almost as soon as it goes into the frying pan. When cooking pan-

cakes you need only a minimum of oil or fat to prevent the pancake sticking. For omelettes, have the butter sufficiently hot to set the beaten eggs almost as soon as they go into the pan.

Poaching – this is a real art, and the various methods are given on page 109. The temperature of the water during cooking is important. If it boils too rapidly the egg white will be puffed up in the air and tends to disintegrate. If the water is not kept at a sufficiently high temperature the egg will not keep a good shape.

Scrambling – may be considered as **simmering,** for the secret is to cook the eggs slowly and not to over-stir.

Successful cheese cookery depends upon the wise choice of cheese – Cheddar, Cheshire, Gouda, Edam, Gruyère and Emmenthal, together with Parmesan, are some of the best cooking varieties. Remember that over-cooking toughens cheese, whether it is part of a sauce or put on toast and grilled.

There are many ways of cooking rice. Cooks often have their own special method, but one of the most successful and simple is given on page 116. Select a long-grain rice for savoury dishes, do not stir too much during cooking and time the boiling and simmering processes accurately.

Use an adequate amount of water when cooking pasta, for this keeps the macaroni, spaghetti or other shapes, from sticking together. The actual quantities are given in the recipes. Pasta should boil steadily during cooking and you lose an appreciable amount of flavour if you over-cook it.

Baked Eggs

Warm 4 ramekins or individual ovenproof dishes and brush all round inside with melted butter. Break 2 eggs into each dish and top with a piece of butter.

Place the ramekins in a baking dish half filled with hot (not boiling) water. Bake in a moderately hot oven (190°C, 375°F, Gas Mark 5) for about 8 minutes, until the whites are just set. Serve at once.

Savoury Baked Eggs

METRIC/IMPERIAL
1 onion
2 tomatoes
50 g/2 oz butter
salt and pepper
4 eggs
2 tablespoons grated cheese

Peel and dice the onion, peel and slice the tomatoes. Heat 40 g/1½ oz butter in 4 ramekins or individual ovenproof dishes. Add the onion and tomato and season well. Bake in a moderately hot oven (190°C, 375°F, Gas Mark 5) for 8 minutes. Add the eggs, a little seasoning, the cheese and remaining butter. Bake for a further 8 minutes. Serve with fingers of toast.

Swiss Eggs

METRIC/IMPERIAL
100 g/4 oz Cheddar cheese
25 g/1 oz butter
4 eggs
salt and pepper
2 tablespoons single cream or top of the milk

1 Grate a quarter of the cheese and with a very sharp knife cut the remainder into wafer thin slices.

2 Spread the butter all over the bottom of a flameproof dish. Cover with the thin slices of cheese.

3 Break the eggs carefully on to the bed of cheese, being careful not to break the yolks. Season with salt and pepper and put a little of the cream or milk on the top of each egg.

4 Sprinkle over the grated cheese. Bake in a hot oven (220°C, 425°F, Gas Mark 7) for 15 minutes or brown under a hot grill.

Boiled Eggs

There are two methods of boiling an egg. In the first, which gives a lighter egg white, the egg is put into cold water and the water brought to the boil. If using this method allow $3\frac{1}{2}$ minutes from the moment the water boils for a lightly set egg, up to 8-10 minutes for a hard-boiled egg. The other method is to put the eggs into boiling water, in which case allow 4 minutes for a lightly set egg, up to 10 minutes for a hard-boiled egg.

Crack the shell of a hard-boiled egg as soon as cooked and put the egg into cold water. This prevents a dark line forming around the yolk.

Hot Devilled Eggs

METRIC/IMPERIAL
1 medium onion
50 g/2 oz butter or margarine
$\frac{1}{2}$ teaspoon made mustard
$\frac{1}{2}$ teaspoon curry powder
salt and pepper
8 eggs, hard-boiled
For the sauce:
25 g/1 oz butter or margarine
25 g/1 oz flour
$\frac{1}{2}$-1 teaspoon curry powder
300 ml/$\frac{1}{2}$ pint milk
few drops of Worcestershire sauce
salt and pepper
For the topping:
50 g/2 oz breadcrumbs
25 g/1 oz butter or margarine

Peel and chop the onion very finely, then fry in the hot butter or margarine. Stir in the mustard, curry powder and seasoning.

Halve the eggs lengthways, remove the yolks and chop and blend with the onion

mixture. Pack into the whites and put cut side downwards in a long shallow dish.

Make a sauce of the butter, flour blended with the curry powder, milk and Worcestershire sauce (see page 84). Taste and season well. Pour very carefully over the eggs. Top with the crumbs and butter or margarine cut into tiny pieces.

Bake in a moderate oven (180°C, 350°F, Gas Mark 4) for 15-20 minutes, until the top is crisp and brown. Or, if preferred, put under a hot grill.

Poached Eggs

Like all egg dishes, poached eggs must be served the moment they are cooked, so if serving with toast it is advisable to toast the bread while the eggs cook.

First method
Crack the shells and pour the eggs into a cup or saucer. If you have a proper egg-poacher put a piece of margarine or butter, about the size of a hazelnut, into each cup, adding a pinch of salt, if wished. Heat the poacher over water – the margarine or butter MUST be hot before the eggs are added. Gradually add the eggs. Put on the lid and allow the water in the pan to boil steadily for about 3½-4 minutes. Slide the eggs on to buttered toast.

Second method
Put a small piece of margarine or butter into an old cup and stand it in a pan of boiling water to melt. Pour in the egg, put a lid on the pan and cook as before.

Third method
This method is preferred by many people as it gives a lighter result. Bring 300 ml/½ pint water to the boil in a saucepan or frying pan. Add 1-2 teaspoons vinegar, if wished, for this prevents the egg whites from spreading. Put in a generous pinch of salt. Slide the eggs into the boiling water and leave for 3 minutes, or until the white is set. Insert a spoon or fish slice, drain the eggs carefully and put on toast.

Eggs Mornay

Make 300 ml/½ pint cheese sauce (see page 84). Poach 4 eggs by any of the methods above and put on buttered toast or in a flameproof dish. Cover with the sauce and sprinkle with grated cheese. Brown quickly under a hot grill.

A Perfect Omelette

Break the eggs into a basin. Allow 3-4 eggs for 2 people. To give a light omelette a small amount of water can be used, and if you rinse out the egg shells with the water, no egg is wasted. Season and beat the eggs lightly.

Heat a good knob of butter in an omelette pan. Allow 25 g/1 oz for a small sized omelette. Pour in the beaten eggs. Allow the egg mixture to set into a thin skin, then, using either a fork or palette knife, push the egg away from the sides, at the same time tilting the omelette pan so the liquid egg from the top falls into the pan.

Put the filling on to one half of the omelette. Take a palette knife and insert it under the omelette, near the handle. Either fold in half or roll slightly; the thickness of the filling determines which you will do. Always fold, or roll, away from the handle.

Hold the hot plate or dish in your left hand and tip the omelette on to this. Serve as quickly as possible.

Pancakes

METRIC/IMPERIAL
15 g/½ oz lard or cooking fat or 2 teaspoons oil
savoury filling
For the batter:
100 g/4 oz plain flour
pinch of salt
1 egg
300 ml/½ pint milk
1 tablespoon oil or melted butter
(optional)

Makes 8-10

First make the batter. Sift the flour and salt into a basin large enough to allow for beating in the liquid. Break the egg into a small basin and then add it to the flour. Add about a quarter of the milk and stir carefully with a wooden spoon until the flour is blended. Beat really hard until it is smooth. Either beat in the rest of the liquid or let the thick batter stand for 10-15 minutes and

then gradually add the rest of the liquid. When the batter becomes thinner, use a flat egg whisk to aerate the mixture. The batter is then ready to use. Add the oil or melted butter just before cooking.

Put the lard, cooking fat or oil into a small pan and heat until a faint haze rises. It is important to have a thin covering of batter only, so pour the batter from a jug or spoon; add only enough to give a paper-thin covering in the pan. Cook steadily on the first side for about 2 minutes, then turn or toss the pancake. Cook for a further 2 minutes on the second side. The pancake is then ready. Either put in the filling at once or remove from the pan and put on a hot dish. After making each pancake, heat a very little extra fat or oil before cooking the next. The pan should have just a thin film of grease.

To keep pancakes hot

When cooked, put each pancake on to a hot dish or plate, or on to a sheet of greaseproof paper covered in castor sugar on a hot dish or plate. Either keep hot in the oven, with the heat turned very low, or keep them hot on a plate over a saucepan of hot water. Serve as quickly as possible.

Savoury fillings for omelettes and pancakes

Cheese: either add grated cheese to the eggs before cooking, or, to give a moister filling, put grated cheese into the omelette just before folding or rolling.

Tomato: fry peeled tomatoes until soft, season well and put most of the tomato mixture into the omelette before folding or rolling. Top the omelette with the remainder.

Prawn or shrimp: heat peeled prawns or shrimps in a little butter or white sauce, and put into the omelette before rolling or folding.

✳ Pancakes freeze well. Always use the oil or melted butter in the batter to give the pancakes a better texture. Separate each pancake with squares of waxed or greaseproof paper before wrapping. Plain pancakes keep for 4-5 months.

Cheese Soufflé

METRIC/IMPERIAL
25 g/1 oz butter or margarine
25 g/1 oz flour
150 ml/¼ pint milk
3 egg yolks
75-100 g/3-4 oz Cheddar cheese, grated
4 egg whites
salt and pepper

Serves 4

1 Heat the butter in a large saucepan. Stir in the flour and cook for several minutes. Gradually add the milk, bring to the boil and cook until thickened. This will produce a really thick sauce (panada) which needs to be stirred vigorously.

2 Beat in the egg yolks and the grated cheese.

3 Whisk the egg whites until very stiff and fold in with a metal spoon. Season to taste. If preferred, the seasoning may be added to the sauce, but adding it later enables it to be adjusted better.

4 Pour into a greased 15-cm/6-inch soufflé dish, flatten on top with a palette knife and bake in a moderately hot oven (190-200°C, 375-400°F, Gas Mark 5-6) for 25-30 minutes until well risen and golden brown. A certain amount of experimenting with oven temperatures may have to be done for perfect baking–a soufflé should not be baked for too long a period otherwise it is dry. Serve at once.

NOTE Other hard cheeses may be used, or use half Cheddar, half Parmesan.

Welsh Rarebit

METRIC/IMPERIAL
25 g/1 oz butter
25 g/1 oz flour
150 ml/¼ pint milk
1 teaspoon made mustard
salt and pepper
225 g/8 oz cheese, grated*
1 tablespoon beer or ale or Worcestershire
sauce
4 large slices bread
Garnish with any of the following:
tomato slices
sardines
mushroom slices
cooked bacon rashers
prunes
pineapple rings

*a Dutch Gouda or Edam makes a soft creamy Welsh rarebit; use Cheddar or Cheshire for a creamy mild flavour; mix in a little Parmesan to give a real 'bite'

Serves 4

Melt the butter in a saucepan, stir in the flour and cook steadily for several minutes, then gradually add the cold milk. Bring to the boil and cook until smooth and thick. Add the mustard, salt, pepper, most of the cheese and the beer. Heat gently, until the cheese has melted.

Meanwhile toast the bread and butter it. Spread the rarebit mixture over the toast, sprinkle with the remainder of the cheese and place under a hot grill for 1-2 minutes. Top with the chosen garnish.

This is the classic soft rarebit. For a less runny mixture slightly reduce the quantity of milk.

The Welsh rarebit mixture can be stored in a covered jar for several days in a refrigerator.

Variations

Tomato rarebit: blend the mixture with tomato juice or soup instead of milk. If using soup, use a little less flour.

Celery rarebit: arrange neat pieces of well drained cooked celery on the toast and coat with the rarebit mixture. The celery stock can be used in place of the milk.

Buck rarebit: top the mixture with a poached egg.

Creole rarebit: mix the rarebit mixture with fried onion and tomatoes and a little sweet corn.

Vegetable rarebit: mix a few cooked well drained vegetables into the rarebit mixture.

Salami rarebit: place a slice of salami on the toast; top with the rarebit mixture and brown under a hot grill. Garnish with a bacon roll, apple slices and a sprig of parsley.

York rarebit: place a thick slice of cooked ham on the toast, then cover with the rarebit mixture.

Croque Monsieur

METRIC/IMPERIAL
8 thin slices bread and butter
4 slices Gruyère cheese
4 slices ham
butter or oil and butter for frying
chopped parsley

Serves 2 or 4

Make sandwiches using the bread and butter, slices of cheese and ham. Cut away the crusts from the bread and cut each sandwich into 2 fingers. Fry the fingers in the hot butter or the oil and butter until they are crisp and golden brown. Garnish with a little chopped parsley.

Cheese Fondue

METRIC/IMPERIAL
25 g/1 oz butter
450 g/1 lb Gruyère cheese, grated (or half Gruyère, half Emmenthal)
salt and pepper
300 ml/$\frac{1}{2}$ pint Graves or other dry white wine
little brandy, curaçao or cider

Serves 4

Butter the bottom and sides of a copper or flameproof dish or flameproof earthenware casserole (unsalted butter is ideal for this). Gradually add the grated cheese, seasoning and wine. Keep warm over a gentle heat and stir from time to time. If desired, add a little brandy, curaçao or cider. Serve cubes of bread to be dipped into the fondue.

Cornflour can be used to prevent the mixture curdling; blend 2 teaspoons cornflour with a little of the wine and add to the fondue.

For a more exotic fondue add a little kirsch. For a milder-flavoured fondue, use Cheddar cheese, but this will not produce a traditional stringy fondue.

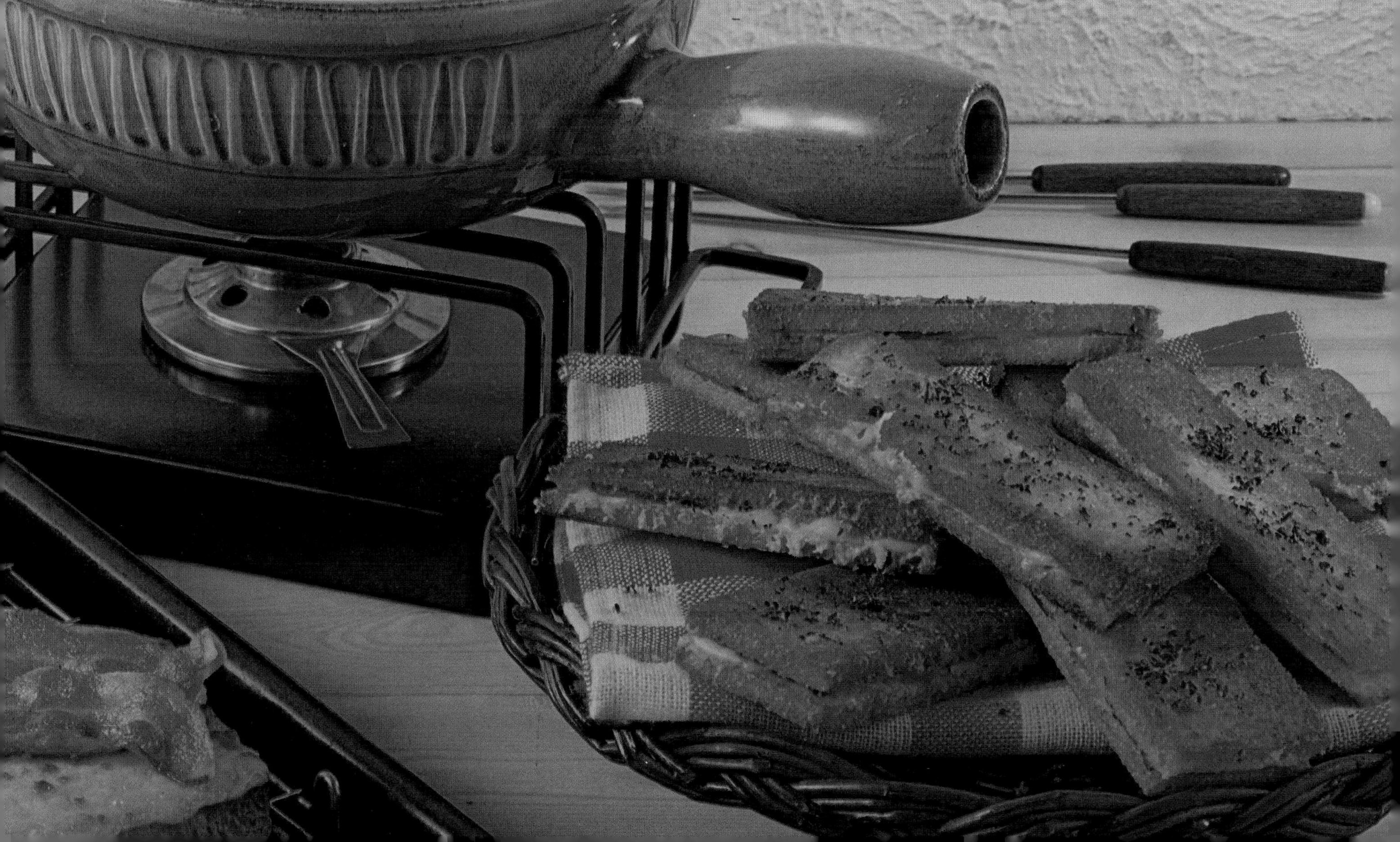

Choosing Rice

Rice, while having the same flavour, varies a great deal in the way it cooks, so choose a long grain of rice (Patna is one type) for savoury dishes where it is particularly important that the rice grains are not sticky; use a short (round) grain rice for sweet puddings to give a creamy texture.

The Three Basic Methods of Cooking Rice

First method

To each 100 g/4 oz rice allow 1.15 litres/2 pints boiling salted water. Put in the rice and cook rapidly for about 15 minutes. Strain, rinse in boiling water and put on to flat trays in a cool oven to dry for a short time.

Second method

Either use a cup measure or a gram/ounce measure, and allow 1 cup rice, 2 cups water; or 100 g/4 oz rice, 250 ml/8 fl oz water. Put the rice, cold water and salt to taste into a saucepan with a tightly fitting lid. Bring to the boil, stir briskly with a fork, put on the lid, lower the heat and simmer gently for 15 minutes. By this time the water will have been absorbed and every grain of rice cooked, but not sticky.

Third method

Use the same proportions as the second method, but put into the top of a double saucepan over boiling water. Cook for approximately 30 minutes with the lid on tightly.

In the second and third methods it is not necessary to rinse the rice.

NOTE: 25 g/1 oz uncooked rice becomes 50-75 g/2-3 oz when cooked.

Risotto

The most simple risotto is made by frying 1 or 2 sliced onions in 50 g/2 oz butter, then adding 225 g/8 oz long-grain rice. Turn this in the butter until translucent and then add approximately 900 ml/1½ pints chicken or beef stock (or use a mixture of both), together with a little white wine and seasoning. Cook in an uncovered pan until the rice has absorbed the liquid, or use just enough liquid to cover the rice and cook in a tightly closed pan. During cooking toss the rice carefully with a fork to separate the grains and, as the liquid evaporates, to prevent the rice sticking to the pan. Before serving add another good knob of butter and 25-50 g/1-2 oz grated Parmesan cheese.

Serve this as a separate dish for 4 people or, although not traditional in Italy, it could be served with meat or poultry.

Risotto alla Finanziera

METRIC/IMPERIAL
1 small onion
100 g/4 oz mushrooms
1 small sweet red pepper
6-8 chicken livers
75 g/3 oz butter
350 g/12 oz long-grain rice
1.75 litres/3 pints chicken stock
salt and pepper
grated Parmesan cheese

Serves 4-6

Chop the onion, mushrooms, red pepper and chicken livers. Melt the butter in a large pan and toss the chopped ingredients in it. Add the rice and cook for about 10 minutes, stirring well. Add the chicken stock, stirring all the time, and then cook steadily in an open pan until the liquid has all been absorbed.

Season generously before serving; a little Marsala could be added if wished. Serve with grated Parmesan cheese.

This dish can be prepared beforehand if the mushrooms are fried separately and added when reheating.

✳ To freeze rice see page 76.

Jambalaya

METRIC/IMPERIAL
1 medium onion
2 sticks celery or chicory
2 tablespoons olive oil
225 g/8 oz cooked long-grain rice
1 (227-g/8-oz) can tomatoes
225 g/8 oz frankfurter sausages or cooked meat
salt and pepper
1 tablespoon chopped parsley
grated Parmesan cheese

Serves 4

Peel and chop the onion and dice the celery or chicory. Heat the oil in a frying pan and cook the prepared vegetables over a gentle heat until soft and golden. Add the rice and stir until thoroughly mixed. Add the tomatoes, sausages, seasoning and parsley. Cook gently for about 20 minutes. Serve very hot with grated Parmesan cheese.

Oriental Chicken and Rice Salad

METRIC/IMPERIAL
175 g/6 oz long-grain rice
1 clove garlic, cut (optional)
3 tablespoons salad oil
1 tablespoon wine or tarragon vinegar
salt and pepper
1 large tomato
1 green pepper
225 g/8 oz cooked chicken
1 tablespoon currants
2 tablespoons chopped walnuts (optional)

Serves 4

Cook the rice by the chosen method. Rub a large bowl with the garlic and in it mix together the oil, vinegar and seasoning.

Peel and chop the tomato and remove the seeds. Finely slice the pepper and cut the chicken into bite-size pieces.

Add the hot rice to the bowl and stir in all the remaining ingredients. Cover and set aside in a cool place for the flavours to blend. When cold, transfer to a serving dish.

Paella Valencia

Paella is one of the most famous Spanish shellfish dishes. Chicken and shellfish are cooked together and its colourful appearance is as interesting as its original flavour. Paella varies, of course, in different parts of Spain. In some places diced fat bacon is added; in others, white fish are put in, in place of the chicken; squid is another ingredient which may be added.

METRIC/IMPERIAL
1 small chicken
1 onion
1 clove garlic
2 tablespoons oil
1.15 litres/2 pints chicken stock
2 medium tomatoes
1 small cooked lobster (optional)
6-8 mussels
1 red pepper
225 g/8 oz long-grain rice
little saffron
4 Dublin Bay prawns or 6-10 large prawns, peeled
225 g/8 oz cooked peas
few unpeeled prawns to garnish

Serves 4

Divide the chicken into neat pieces. Peel the onion and garlic and chop very finely. Fry the chicken, onion and garlic in the oil in a large open pan until golden. Add half the stock and simmer for 10-15 minutes.

Meanwhile peel and coarsely chop the tomatoes. Divide the lobster into pieces and clean the mussels thoroughly. Remove the seeds from the pepper and chop. Add the tomatoes, rice and remaining stock to the pan. Simmer for 5 minutes and stir in the saffron. Add the lobster pieces, mussels, pepper, prawns and peas, arranging the seafood in an attractive pattern in the pan.

Continue cooking for a further 15-20 minutes, until the rice is cooked and has absorbed most of the liquid. Discard any mussels which have not opened. Garnish the dish with the unpeeled prawns.

Choosing Pasta

Pasta is the name used to describe the macaroni foods, which include spaghetti, cannelloni, etc. Choosing it is quite a problem, since there are so many varieties . . . for example ravioli and cannelloni (both forms of pasta which are stuffed), wheels and shells (often cooked to serve instead of potatoes), vermicelli and seed pasta (frequently just used to garnish soups), ribbon, twisted and green noodles – used in many dishes. Many pasta shapes are interchangeable, since they have the same flavour and result in cooking.

Cooking Pasta

It is very important to make sure that the pasta is put into a sufficient quantity of boiling salted water. If you use too little water it becomes sticky and is inadequately cooked. Use at least 1.15 litres/2 pints water to 100 g/4 oz pasta.

Do not over-cook. The pasta is cooked when it feels just tender (*al dente*), and if you take a piece out there should be no white uncooked flour on it. Serve as soon as possible after cooking.

There are varieties of quick-cooking pasta on the market and these are of good quality. Their shape has just been adjusted to make them cook more rapidly.

Spaghetti Marinara

METRIC/IMPERIAL
225 g/8 oz spaghetti
1 onion
450 g/1 lb tomatoes
100 g/4 oz mushrooms
1 (56-g/2-oz) can anchovy fillets
1 tablespoon oil
salt and pepper
2 bay leaves
4 rashers bacon
grated Parmesan cheese to garnish

Serves 4

Half fill a large saucepan with water and bring to the boil, adding a good teaspoon of salt. Drop in the spaghetti, bring back to the boil and cook steadily for 10 minutes, no longer. Drain thoroughly and keep warm.

While the spaghetti is cooking prepare the rest of the mixture. Peel and slice the onion and tomatoes. Slice the mushrooms. Drain off the oil from the anchovies and put this, together with the other tablespoon of oil, into a large saucepan. When this is hot, fry the onion, tomatoes and mushrooms until they form a soft sauce. Drain the spaghetti and add to the sauce. Add seasoning to taste, remembering that the anchovies will make it very salty, and the bay leaves. Simmer gently for 10-15 minutes, adding most of the anchovies during the last 5 minutes.

Cut the bacon into small dice and fry until crisp and brown.

Remove the bay leaves and pile the spaghetti mixture into a hot dish. Garnish with the remaining anchovies, pieces of bacon and grated cheese.

Spaghetti alla Bolognese

METRIC/IMPERIAL
225 g/8 oz spaghetti
grated Parmesan cheese
For the sauce:
50 g/2 oz mushrooms
1 onion
1 tablespoon oil
450 g/1 lb minced raw beef
2-3 teaspoons concentrated tomato purée
1 (396-g/14-oz) can Italian tomatoes
salt and pepper
150 ml/¼ pint beef stock
4 tablespoons red wine
1 bay leaf

Serves 4 as a main dish

Finely chop the mushrooms. Peel and thinly slice the onion. Heat the oil in a heavy pan and add the onion. Cook for a few minutes until tender. Add the meat and cook, stirring, until the meat is browned. Then add the mushrooms and the remaining ingredients. Bring to the boil, cover with a lid, reduce the heat and simmer gently, stirring occasionally, for 45 minutes.

About 15 minutes before the sauce is ready, cook the spaghetti. Put into a large pan of boiling salted water. Bring back to the boil and cook for 10-12 minutes. Drain the spaghetti and put on to hot plates or dishes. Top with the sauce and sprinkle with Parmesan cheese.

❋ The sauce freezes well for 3 months. Cooked spaghetti tends to lose texture in freezing.

Spaghetti with Tomato and Pepper Sauce

METRIC/IMPERIAL
1 onion
225 g/8 oz tomatoes
1 small red or green pepper
2 tablespoons oil
½–1 clove garlic
100 g/4 oz cooked pork, minced
2 tablespoons chopped parsley
little hot water or stock
salt and pepper
225 g/8 oz spaghetti
grated Parmesan or Pecorino cheese

Serves 4

Peel and chop the onion and tomatoes and slice the red or green pepper. Heat the oil in a pan and brown the garlic, onion and pork. Remove the garlic and add the tomatoes, red pepper and parsley. Cook for 5 minutes before adding sufficient hot water or stock to make a sauce. Add the seasoning last. Simmer until the tomatoes are reduced to a pulp, stirring occasionally. The longer you cook the better the flavour, but make sure the sauce does not become too dry.

Cook the spaghetti in a large saucepan half full of boiling salted water for 10 minutes. Drain and mix well with a little of the grated cheese. Pour the sauce over and sprinkle with the remaining cheese.

or leave whole. Separate the layers and lay flat on a sheet of damp greaseproof paper. Make the Bolognese sauce.

Put a layer of the lasagne into a buttered dish, then a layer of sauce, then a little cream cheese, Parmesan cheese and Gruyère cheese. Fill the dish like this, ending with the Parmesan and Gruyère cheese. Bake in the centre of a moderately hot oven (200°C, 400°F, Gas Mark 6) for about 30 minutes.

Variation

For a moister lasagne, substitute 300 ml/½ pint cheese sauce (see page 84) for the various cheeses.

✳ The cooked lasagne dish freezes well for 3 months. If making the variation with cheese sauce there is no need to pre-cook the pasta. Layer uncooked pasta with the sauces and freeze.

Lasagne

METRIC/IMPERIAL
175 g/6 oz lasagne
Bolognese sauce (see Spaghetti alla Bolognese, page 121)
100 g/4 oz cream cheese
50 g/2 oz Parmesan cheese, grated
100-150 g/4-5 oz Gruyère cheese, thinly sliced

Serves 3-4

This wide ribbon type of pasta forms the basis for many delicious dishes. You can obtain the green spinach-flavoured lasagne as well as the plain pasta. Always use plenty of boiling salted water and a very large pan. Either break into convenient pieces or lower one end of the long sticks into the boiling salted water, and wait for this to soften before allowing the rest of the pasta to go into the saucepan.

Cook the lasagne in boiling salted water for about 20-25 minutes until tender. Drain and rinse well. Cut into convenient lengths

Macaroni Cheese

METRIC/IMPERIAL
175 g/6 oz macaroni
salt
600 ml/1 pint cheese sauce (see page 84)
50 g/2 oz Cheddar or Gruyère cheese, grated
1 tablespoon crisp breadcrumbs
25 g/1 oz margarine or butter
tomato slices to garnish

Serves 4

Cook the macaroni in boiling salted water, until just tender. Do not overcook; elbow quick cooking macaroni takes 7 minutes only. Drain in a colander, arrange in a hot dish and pour the cheese sauce over. Sprinkle cheese and breadcrumbs on top and dot with the margarine or butter. Either bake near the top of a moderately hot oven (200°C, 400°F, Gas Mark 6) for about 25 minutes until crisp and brown, or put under a hot grill. Garnish with tomato slices.

Baking

Secrets of Success

Baking is a method of cooking a wide variety of savoury and sweet dishes, many of which need special techniques in blending the ingredients.

The most important factor to consider first is your oven. Each oven is individual in the way it heats. Manufacturers take great trouble to check thermostats and ensure the even cooking of food, but oven temperatures can vary slightly between models. This is why you should always check recommended settings in recipes against your manufacturer's own instruction book or card.

The position in which the food is placed in the oven will have an effect upon the cooking. Large cakes, loaves, deep pies and tarts and anything wanting steady cooking should be placed in the centre of the oven, unless instructed otherwise. Small cakes, scones or anything fairly shallow, which will cook through more rapidly, can be placed in the hotter area above the centre, or below the centre in certain electric ovens.

If you use a different sized container from that suggested in the recipe you will need to alter the cooking time. A larger tin or dish means the mixture is spread out over a greater area, and being more shallow will, therefore, cook more rapidly. On the other hand a smaller tin or dish means a greater depth of mixture which could extend the cooking time. This may well mean you need to use a slightly lower setting than that given in the recipe, or reduce the heat after part of the cooking time.

The various techniques of mixing dealt with in this chapter are:

Rubbing-in – the fat is incorporated into the flour with the tips of your fingers. Avoid over-handling the mixture.

Creaming – the fat and sugar are beaten together until smooth, soft and light in texture. Follow the directions on adding eggs and flour carefully, see page 132.

Melting – a quick and easy way to combine liquid and fat, plus sweetening in many recipes. It is not only the initial stage in preparing moist gingerbread, but also choux pastry. When making this pastry incorporate the flour carefully, as outlined in the recipe on page 144.

Folding – a term used when making very light sponges. After whisking the eggs and sugar until thick and light it is *essential* to fold in the sifted flour gently and carefully. Folding is a gentle turning and flicking movement. This word also describes the way the richer pastry doughs, such as flaky, are folded to incorporate the fat and air.

Kneading – a term used when preparing the dough in yeast cookery. The way this is kneaded plays an important part in producing light-textured bread, so follow the directions on page 176.

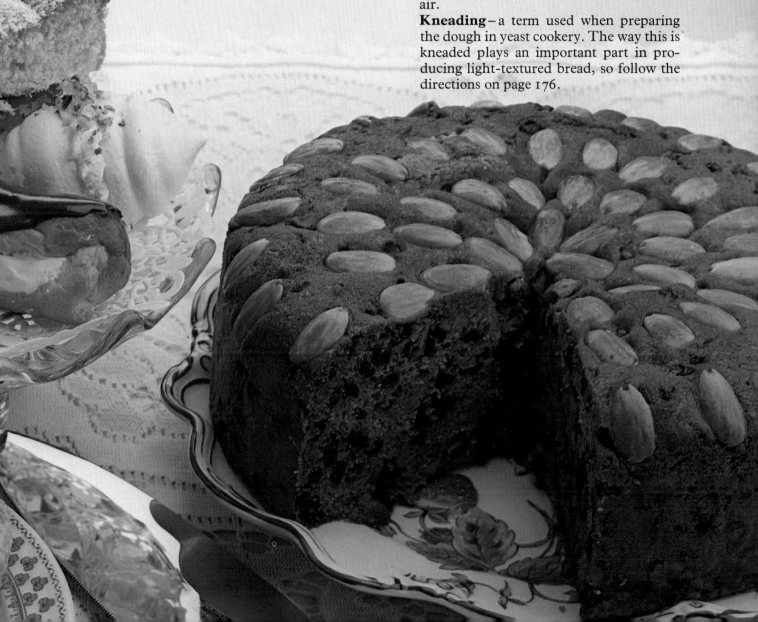

Short Crust Pastry

It is important to note that where a recipe says 225 g/8 oz short crust pastry, it means pastry made with 225 g/8 oz flour.

For a richer short crust bind with an egg yolk. For sweet short crust pastry add 15-25 g/½-1 oz sugar to the pastry mixture after the fat has been rubbed in.

METRIC/IMPERIAL
225 g/8 oz plain flour
pinch of salt
110 g/4 oz fat (half butter or margarine
and half lard or cooking fat)★
2-3 tablespoons cold water
★if using all vegetable fat or lard the
quantity can be reduced to 75-90 g/3-3½ oz

1 Sift the flour and salt together. Rub in the fat, using the fingertips, until the mixture resembles fine breadcrumbs. Rub quickly and lightly, lifting the mixture up all the time to incorporate as much cool air as possible.

2 Sprinkle the water evenly over the mixture. With a palette knife or any round-bladed kitchen knife, mix together lightly, cutting through and pressing together. Bind together to a firm dough using the fingers.

Place the dough on a lightly floured board and remove cracks by kneading gently. Flour the rolling pin lightly and, using short, sharp strokes, roll the pastry to the required thickness and lightness. Roll in one direction only and turn as necessary.

✳ The pastry can be formed into a neat shape, wrapped and frozen for 5-6 months.

Cornish Pasties

METRIC/IMPERIAL
275 g/10 oz short crust pastry
175 g/6 oz good quality stewing or rump
steak
2 medium potatoes
1 large onion
salt and pepper
dry mustard
3 tablespoons stock or gravy or water
flavoured with a little yeast extract
milk or beaten egg to glaze

Serves 4

Roll the pastry out to about 5 mm/¼ inch thick, then cut into four rounds about the size of a large tea-plate.

Cut the meat into tiny pieces. Peel and dice the potatoes and onion. Mix these together and add seasoning. Put a good pile in the centre of each round of pastry and moisten with a little of the stock. Brush the edges of the pastry with water, then bring these together in the centre.

Press them tightly so that there is no possibility of their opening during cooking, and stand the pasties on a baking tray. Brush over with either a little milk or beaten egg to give a slight glaze.

Bake in the centre of a hot oven (220°C, 425°F, Gas Mark 7) for 25 minutes. Lower the heat to moderate (180°C, 350°F, Gas Mark 4) for a further 25-35 minutes, to make sure the meat is cooked inside.

✳ Cooked pasties can be frozen for 3 months.

Quiche Lorraine

METRIC/IMPERIAL
2-3 rashers bacon
175 g/6 oz short crust pastry
2 eggs
150 ml/¼ pint single cream
150 ml/¼ pint milk
175 g/6 oz cheese, grated
salt and pepper
To garnish:
parsley
tomato quarters

Serves 4

Chop the bacon finely and fry very lightly. Line a 20-cm/8-inch flan ring with the pastry. Beat together the eggs, cream, milk, grated cheese, bacon and seasoning. Pour carefully into the flan case and bake in the centre of a moderately hot oven (200°C, 400°F, Gas Mark 6) for 30-40 minutes, until the pastry is cooked and the filling firm. Garnish with parsley and tomato quarters.

NOTE: To give a crisper pastry, bake the pastry 'blind' as in the Custard Tart, then add the filling, lower the heat and cook for 35-40 minutes.

❋ The cooked quiche freezes well for 3 months.

Variations

Bacon quiche: halfway through cooking place thin bacon strips on top of the quiche, in a lattice design. Return to the oven to finish cooking. Garnish with stuffed olives.

Corn quiche: mix in 1 (198-g/7-oz) can drained sweet corn with the eggs, but reduce the cheese to 75 g/3 oz. Garnish with parsley and tomato quarters.

Custard Tart

METRIC/IMPERIAL
150 g/5 oz short crust pastry
2 eggs or 1 egg and 1 egg yolk
1 tablespoon sugar
300 ml/½ pint hot milk
little grated nutmeg

Serves 6

Line an 18-cm/7-inch flan ring or tin with the pastry. Bake the pastry 'blind' in a hot oven (220°C, 425°F, Gas Mark 7) for 10 minutes to set the bottom. To bake 'blind', line the pastry case with foil or greaseproof paper cut to shape and weigh down with dried beans.

Beat the eggs and sugar and pour over the hot, not boiling, milk. Pour into the pastry case, then bake in the centre of a moderate oven (180°C, 350°F, Gas Mark 4) for a further 20 minutes. When set, top with grated nutmeg.

The pastry and custard can also be baked together, in which case:

Line a flan tin or ring with pastry. Brush liberally with egg white to prevent it rising. Pour in the egg custard mixture, using cold milk. Bake in a moderate oven (180°C, 350°F, Gas Mark 4) for 35-35 minutes. Top with grated nutmeg.

Fruit Pie

METRIC/IMPERIAL
175 g/6 oz short crust or sweet short crust
pastry
450 g/1 lb fruit
50-100 g/2-4 oz sugar (depending on fruit
used)
2-4 tablespoons water

Serves 4

Put a pie funnel in the centre of a pie dish. Prepare the fruit and put into the pie dish with the sugar and water. Hard fruit (apples, firm plums, etc.) need the larger amount of water; soft fruit (blackcurrants, etc.) the smaller amount. Add any extra flavouring, e.g. 2-3 cloves or a little lemon rind and lemon juice, to the apples.

Roll out the pastry; this must be bigger than the top of the pie dish to allow for a narrow strip to be cut off. Press this on the dampened rim of the dish. Brush with a little water. Lay the pastry over the top. Cut away the surplus, press the edges of the pastry together firmly and decorate.

Stand the pie on a baking tray and bake in the centre of a hot oven (220°C, 425°F, Gas Mark 7) for 10-15 minutes. Reduce the heat to moderate (180°C, 350°F, Gas Mark 4) for a further 20 minutes for soft fruit, and 30 minutes for hard fruit. Sprinkle with castor sugar before serving.

Fillings for Fruit Pies

Use any fruit that is in season; the following are particularly interesting ways to vary fruit pies. There are many canned fruit pie fillings which can be used in place of fresh fruit.

Apple and raisin pie: add 100 g/4 oz seedless raisins to each 450 g/1 lb apples. If the raisins are fairly dry, heat for a few minutes in water, then use this liquid in the pie. Add normal amount of sugar.

Apple and prune pie: allow 100 g/4 oz dried prunes to each 450 g/1 lb apples. Soak in water or water and orange juice to cover overnight, unless sufficiently tender to omit this step. Put with the apples in the pie dish, or if rather hard simmer gently for a time, then add to the apples and sugar.

Cherry and almond pie: add about 50-75 g/2-3 oz blanched almonds to each 450 g/1 lb cherries.

✳ Fruit pies freeze well for 3 months.

Plain Scones

METRIC/IMPERIAL
225 g/8 oz flour*
generous pinch of salt
25-50 g/1-2 oz margarine
25 g/1 oz sugar
150 ml/¼ pint milk
*with plain flour use 1 teaspoon cream of tartar and ½ teaspoon bicarbonate of soda. With self-raising flour use 1 teaspoon baking powder for lighter scones

Makes 12

Sift together the flour, salt, bicarbonate of soda and cream of tartar. Rub in the margarine and add the sugar. Mix to a soft rolling consistency with the milk. Roll out and cut into rounds using a 7.5-cm/2½-inch cutter.

Put on to an ungreased baking tray and bake near the top of a very hot oven (230°C, 450°F, Gas Mark 8) for approximately 10 minutes. To test if cooked press firmly at the sides. Scones are cooked when they feel firm to the touch.

❋ These freeze well for 3 months.

Rock Buns

METRIC/IMPERIAL
225 g/8 oz flour (with plain flour use 1 teaspoon baking powder)
110 g/4 oz margarine or cooking fat
110 g/4 oz sugar
110 g/4 oz mixed dried fruit
2 eggs
little milk
sugar for coating

Makes 10-12

Sift the flour and baking powder, if used, into a large bowl. Rub in the fat until the mixture resembles breadcrumbs.

Add the sugar and dried fruit. Stir in the eggs, using a palette knife. Stir the milk in gradually. The mixture should drop from the knife if shaken very sharply.

Take up small portions of mixture between two forks. Put on to greased flat baking trays, allowing plenty of room for the cakes to spread. Sprinkle with sugar before baking, if wished, or this can be done after baking.

Bake near the top of a hot oven (220°C, 425°F, Gas Mark 7) for 12-15 minutes. If baking two trays of buns, you may need to change them round halfway through cooking, or move the lower tray up in the oven after removing the top tray.

Cool for 2-3 minutes on the tray, as the buns are very crisp and short. Sprinkle with sugar, if not already coated before baking, and lift on to a wire cooling tray.

❋ Freeze for 3 months.

Luncheon Cake

METRIC/IMPERIAL
225 g/8 oz flour (with plain flour use
1 teaspoon baking powder)
150 g/5 oz margarine or 75 g/3 oz
margarine and 50 g/2 oz lard
110-150 g/4-5 oz sugar
175 g/6 oz mixed dried fruit
50 g/2 oz mixed peel
1 egg
little milk
25 g/1 oz almonds (optional)
4 glacé cherries, halved (optional)

Sift the flour and baking powder, if used, into a bowl and rub in the margarine, or margarine and lard. Add the sugar, dried fruit and peel, then the beaten egg and enough milk to make a sticky consistency. Put into a well greased and floured 1-kg/2-lb loaf tin and bake in the centre of a moderate oven (180°C, 350°F, Gas Mark 4) for 1 hour. If using almonds and cherries, blanch and dry the almonds then put on top of the cake with the cherries, before baking.

❋ Freeze for 3 months.

Victoria Sandwich

METRIC/IMPERIAL
110 g/4 oz flour (with plain flour use
1½ teaspoons baking powder)
110 g/4 oz margarine or butter
110 g/4 oz castor sugar
2 large eggs

1 Sift the flour and baking powder, if used. Cream the fat and sugar until soft and white.

2 Break the eggs into a cup to ensure each one is fresh before beating thoroughly in a basin. Add a little of the beaten egg to the creamed mixture and beat until thoroughly blended.

3 Add more egg and beat again – continue until all the egg is used. If the mixture shows any sign of curdling, stir in a little flour. Fold in the remaining flour using a metal spoon.

4 Grease and flour two 18-cm/7-inch sandwich tins and divide the mixture equally between them. Spread slightly away from the centre so that the two halves will be flat.

Bake in a moderate oven (180°C, 350°F, Gas Mark 4) for 18-20 minutes. If using a gas oven, put the tins side by side on a shelf near the top of the oven, or put one under the other. With an electric oven or solid fuel, put one about the second rung from the top and one the second rung from the bottom, or have the tins side by side on the same shelf.

First look to see if the cake has shrunk slightly from the sides of the tin, then test by pressing gently but firmly on top and if no impression is left by the finger the cake is ready to come out of the oven. Wait about 2 minutes for the cakes to set.

Turn out of the tins on to a wire tray. It is quite a good idea to give the tins a sharp tap on the table to loosen the cakes away from the sides and bottom of the tins before attempting to turn them out.

Other flavourings for a Victoria sandwich

Care must be taken that when you add flavour you do not spoil the consistency. For example, in a chocolate cake, because you add cocoa your liquid content must be higher, so put in a little extra liquid. On the other hand, if you add coffee essence, etc., you must use a little extra flour.

If you wish to give an orange or lemon flavour, remember the finely grated rind adds flavour without spoiling the balance of the recipe.

Chocolate: omit 25 g/1 oz flour and use 75 g/3 oz flour and 25 g/1 oz chocolate powder or use 90 g/3½ oz flour and 15 g/½ oz cocoa.

Coffee: blend 1 tablespoon coffee essence with the margarine and sugar; or sift 2-3 teaspoons instant coffee powder with the flour.

Lemon or orange: blend the grated rind of 1-2 lemons or oranges with the margarine or butter and sugar. Add 1 tablespoon fruit juice at the end.

❋ A Victoria sandwich can be frozen for 3 months.

Butter Icing

METRIC/IMPERIAL
50 g/2 oz butter
100 g/4 oz icing sugar, sifted (to make a firmer icing use the larger quantity of sugar)
flavouring as individual recipe or as below

Cream the butter until very soft and white – it is essential not to warm it. Work in the sugar and flavouring.

This is enough for a thick layer through the centre of an 18-cm/7-inch cake. Use double the amount for filling and topping, but at least three times the amount if coating the sides as well. If piping is added allow four times the amount.

Almond and other essences: may be creamed with the butter, etc.
Chocolate: add a small quantity of sifted cocoa or chocolate powder blended with a little hot water to the creamed butter, etc.
Coffee: use a small quantity of concentrated coffee essence or instant coffee powder blended with water.

Amounts to use
For top of an 18-cm/7-inch cake: 100 g/4 oz icing sugar, etc.
For top and sides of an 18-cm/7-inch cake: good 225 g/8 oz icing sugar, etc.

Flavourings to add for water icing
Based on 225 g/8 oz icing sugar, etc.
Almond and other essences: a few drops.
Chocolate: 1 tablespoon sifted cocoa, 7 g/½ oz melted butter, to keep gloss, or 50 g/2 oz melted chocolate.
Mocha: add cocoa or chocolate, mix with coffee essence or blended instant coffee instead of water.
Orange or lemon: mix with either juice instead of water.
Coffee: use strong coffee instead of water – coffee essence or dissolved instant coffee.
Spiced: add a good pinch of ground spice. Colour water icing with a few drops of colouring.

Water Icing or Glacé Icing

This icing is the easiest to make and ideal for covering small cakes, biscuits and light cakes. It cannot be used for piping except for a flowing design, i.e. 'writing' or feathering. It has a tendency to crack after a day or so.

To make
Blend 225 g/8 oz sifted icing sugar with approximately 2-3 tablespoons warm water – for fragile cakes make the icing fairly runny.

Pineapple Layer Cake

METRIC/IMPERIAL
1 Victoria sandwich
butter icing
pineapple essence
glacé pineapple
glacé cherries
glacé icing

Make the Victoria sandwich, and when cooked and cool sandwich the two halves together with the butter icing, flavoured with a little pineapple essence. Add a layer of chopped glacé pineapple and cherries on top of the butter icing.

Cover the cake with glacé icing, again flavoured with pineapple essence. Pipe a border of pineapple-flavoured butter icing at the bottom and decorate with pieces of glacé pineapple and glacé cherries.

Chocolate Fancies

METRIC/IMPERIAL
75 g/3 oz flour (with plain flour use 1 teaspoon baking powder)
25 g/1 oz cocoa
100 g/4 oz butter or margarine
100 g/4 oz sugar
2 eggs
1 tablespoon warm water to mix
glacé icing
butter icing
glacé cherries to decorate

Sift the flour, baking powder if used and cocoa. Cream the butter or margarine and sugar until light and fluffy. Beat the eggs and gradually beat into the butter and sugar.

Fold in the sifted flour mixture and the warm water to give a soft, dropping consistency. Put the mixture into a greased and lined 28 × 17-cm/11 × 7-inch Swiss roll tin and cook in a moderate oven (180°C, 350°F, Gas Mark 4) for about 20 minutes.

When cold cut into fancy shapes. Coat with glacé icing and pipe a border of butter icing round the edge. Decorate with glacé cherries.

Spiced Pear Upside-Down Pudding

METRIC/IMPERIAL
For the topping:
25 g/1 oz soft margarine
25 g/1 oz soft brown sugar
4 canned pear halves
4 canned or glacé cherries
For the pudding mixture:
100 g/4 oz soft margarine
2 eggs
100 g/4 oz soft brown sugar
100 g/4 oz self-raising flour
1 teaspoon baking powder
1 rounded teaspoon ground cinnamon

Grease an 18-cm/7-inch square cake tin and line the bottom with a piece of grease-proof paper.

To make the topping: cream the margarine with the brown sugar. Spread the creamed mixture on the bottom of the tin and arrange the pears on top of this, flat-side downwards.

To make the one-stage pudding: mix all the ingredients together in a mixing bowl, then beat well with a wooden spoon for 1 minute. Spread the mixture on top of the pears and smooth the top of the mixture carefully.

Bake in the centre of a moderate oven (180°C, 350°F, Gas Mark 4) for 40-50 minutes. Test to see if cooked by pressing firmly on top. Look at the pudding after about 25 minutes, and if becoming rather brown reduce the heat to 160°C, 325°F, Gas Mark 3.

Remove from the oven, turn on to a hot dish and place a cherry in the centre of each pear.

Serve hot with cream or custard.

✳ Freeze for 3 months.

Rich Cherry Cake

METRIC/IMPERIAL
175 g/6 oz butter
175 g/6 oz castor sugar
3 large eggs
175 g/6 oz plain flour
½ teaspoon baking powder
50 g/2 oz ground almonds
100 g/4 oz glacé cherries

Cream the butter and sugar until soft and fluffy. Beat the eggs and add gradually to the creamed butter mixture. If the mixture shows signs of curdling, add a little flour.

Sift the flour and baking powder and mix with the ground almonds. Halve the glacé cherries and toss in the flour mixture, then fold the flour mixture and cherries into the butter and egg mixture.

Put into a greased and floured 18-cm/7-inch cake tin and bake in a cool oven (150°C, 300°F, Gas Mark 2) for about 1¾-2 hours until firm to the touch. Turn out carefully.

NOTE: By using a very small amount of baking powder the cherries do not drop in this mixture, but do not add liquid or increase the eggs. The cake does not rise much but keeps beautifully moist.

❄ Freeze for 3 months.

Dundee Cake

METRIC/IMPERIAL
175 g/6 oz butter or margarine
175 g/6 oz castor sugar
3 eggs
225 g/8 oz plain flour
1 teaspoon ground mixed spice
50 g/2 oz glacé cherries
50 g/2 oz chopped almonds
450 g/1 lb mixed dried fruit
50 g/2 oz chopped candied peel
2 tablespoons milk
50 g/2 oz split almonds
To glaze:
egg white left in egg shells

Cream the butter or margarine and sugar together until soft and light. Add the beaten egg. Sift the flour and spice together and stir into the creamed mixture with enough milk to make a slow dropping consistency.

Flour the cherries and mix with the chopped almonds, fruit and peel. Fold into the cake mixture.

Put into a greased and floured 20-cm/8-inch cake tin. Cover with the split almonds and brush with a little egg white to glaze.

Bake in the centre of a moderate oven (160°C, 325°F, Gas Mark 3) for 2-2½ hours, reducing the heat after 1½ hours to 150°C, 300°F, Gas Mark 2. Cool slightly in the tin before turning on to a wire tray.

This cake keeps well in an airtight tin for several weeks.

❄ Can be frozen for 3 months.

Dark Rich Christmas Cake

METRIC/IMPERIAL
100 g/4 oz glacé cherries
575 g/1¼ lb currants
350 g/12 oz sultanas
225 g/8 oz seedless raisins
100 g/4 oz blanched almonds
100 g/4 oz candied peel
275 g/10 oz butter
275 g/10 oz moist brown sugar
1 tablespoon black treacle
grated rind of 1 lemon
grated rind of 1 orange
5 large eggs
2 tablespoons brandy or sherry
350 g/12 oz plain flour
½ teaspoon ground cinnamon
½ teaspoon grated nutmeg
½ teaspoon ground mixed spice
To decorate:
marzipan
royal icing

First prepare the fruit. Wash the glacé cherries in warm water to remove the syrup and wipe dry. If necessary, wash the currants, sultanas and raisins thoroughly and allow to dry completely.

Chop the raisins, almonds and candied peel.

Prepare a 20-cm/8-inch square or a 23-cm/9-inch round cake tin, at least 7.5 cm/3 inches deep, lined with double greaseproof paper at the bottom and sides and a band of brown paper round the outside.

Cream the butter and moist brown sugar with the black treacle and lemon and orange rind. Continue beating until the mixture is soft and light. Whisk the eggs and liquid and gradually beat into the creamed butter mixture, adding a little sifted flour if it shows signs of curdling.

Sift the flour and spices together. In this recipe you do not need any raising agent. Mix the prepared fruit with the almonds and candied peel. Fold thoroughly into the cake with the flour and spices.

Put the mixture into the prepared cake tin and bake in the centre of a moderate oven (160°C, 325°F, Gas Mark 3) for 1½ hours; then lower to cool (140°C, 275°F, Gas Mark 1) for a further 3 hours. Look at the cake after 1 hour at the lower temperature; it should be golden in colour. Cover with foil if becoming too brown. If it is any darker at this stage, lower the temperature again. Test to see if cooked by pressing firmly then listening – an uncooked rich fruit cake makes a distinct 'humming' sound which stops when it is cooked – or insert a skewer into the centre of the cake. If it comes out clean the cake is cooked.

Leave to cool completely in the tin, then turn out carefully on to a wire tray.

Cover with marzipan and rough ice. Decorate with sprigs of holly and stars.

Almond Paste or Marzipan

For top only of a 23-cm/9-inch round cake or 20-cm/8-inch square cake

175 g/6 oz ground almonds
75 g/3 oz castor sugar
100 g/4 oz icing sugar, sifted
few drops of almond essence*
$1\frac{1}{2}$ egg yolks to mix

For top and sides of a 23-cm/9-inch round cake or 20-cm/8-inch square cake (thin layer):

350 g/12 oz ground almonds
175 g/6 oz castor sugar
175 g/6 oz icing sugar, sifted
few drops of almond essence*
3 egg yolks to mix

*The amount of almond essence should, of course, be increased proportionately

Mix all the ingredients together, adding enough egg yolk to make a firm mixture. Knead thoroughly. Do not over-handle.

Royal Icing

To give a somewhat softer icing omit a little egg white and use water instead or 1 teaspoon glycerine to each 225 g/8 oz icing sugar.

For top only of a 23-cm/9-inch round or 20-cm/8-inch square cake – one layer and piping:

$1\frac{1}{2}$ egg whites
350 g/12 oz icing sugar, sifted
$1\frac{1}{4}$ tablespoons lemon juice

For top and sides of a 23-cm/9-inch round or 20-cm/8-inch square cake – one layer and piping:

4 egg whites
900 g/2 lb icing sugar, sifted
2 tablespoons lemon juice

Whisk the egg whites lightly, stir in the icing sugar and lemon juice and beat well until very white and smooth.

Easter Biscuits

METRIC/IMPERIAL
110 g/4 oz butter or margarine
110 g/4 oz castor sugar
225 g/8 oz plain flour or only 175 g/6 oz
for richer biscuits
100 g/4 oz dried fruit
½–1 teaspoon ground mixed spice
little egg yolk or milk to mix

Makes about 10

Cream the butter or margarine and sugar until soft. Work in the flour, fruit and spice. Knead well, then add enough egg or milk to bind the mixture.

Roll out to 5 mm/¼ inch thick, cut into large rounds, put on baking trays and bake in the centre of a moderate oven (180°C, 350°F, Gas Mark 4) for about 15 minutes. Cool on the trays.

Orange Madeleines

METRIC/IMPERIAL
75 g/3 oz margarine
75 g/3 oz castor sugar
2 teaspoons finely grated orange rind
1 egg
110 g/4 oz flour (with plain flour use ½
teaspoon baking powder)
2 tablespoons orange juice
orange marmalade
desiccated coconut
12 crystallised orange slices (optional)

Makes 12–16

Cream the margarine, sugar and orange rind together until soft and light. Add the beaten egg and then fold in the flour, baking powder, if used, and orange juice.

Half fill well greased and floured dariole moulds and bake in a hot oven (220°C, 425°F, Gas Mark 7) for about 10 minutes.

Turn out and brush with warm marmalade, sieved if liked. Roll in coconut and top with a butterfly made by cutting an orange slice in half.

✳ Freeze for 3 months.

Fleur or Flan Pastry or Biscuit Crust

(for sweet flans and fruit tarts)

METRIC/IMPERIAL
110-150 g/4-5 oz butter or margarine
1½ tablespoons sugar
225 g/8 oz plain flour
pinch of salt
cold water or 1 egg yolk to bind

Cream the butter or margarine and sugar together until light in colour. Sift the flour and salt together and add the creamed margarine, mixing with a knife. Gradually add enough water or egg and water to make a firm rolling consistency.

Bind the mixture to a firm dough, using the fingertips. When the dough rolls into a ball without undue pressure, it is the right consistency.

Bake in a moderately hot oven (200°C, 400°F, Gas Mark 6).

To line a flan: put the pastry over the flan tin and press down base and sides firmly, without stretching the pastry, then roll over the top with a rolling pin for a good edge.

French Apple Flan

METRIC/IMPERIAL
6 large cooking apples
150 ml/¼ pint water
100 g/4 oz sugar
2 tablespoons butter
175 g/6 oz short crust (see page 126)
or fleur pastry
4 small cooking or dessert apples
apricot jam to glaze

Serves 4-6

Peel, core and quarter the 6 cooking apples and put in a saucepan with the water, half the sugar and the butter. Cover tightly and cook the apples over moderate heat until tender.

Press the apples through a fine sieve, or purée them in an electric blender and let the purée cool.

Line a 20-cm/8-inch flan ring with pastry and half fill with apple purée. Then peel, core and finely slice the small cooking or dessert apples and arrange the slices over the apple purée in a spiral, starting at the centre and working out, slices overlapping.

Sprinkle the fruit with the rest of the sugar and bake the flan in a moderately hot oven (200°C, 400°F, Gas Mark 6) for 25-30 minutes, or until the apples are tender and the crust is golden. Dessert apples cook without losing their firm texture.

Glaze the hot flan with apricot jam, melted and thinned to a spreading consistency with a little hot water. Top with thick cream if liked.

Lemon Cheesecake

Cheese cakes vary a great deal. This is a particularly good one, with the bite of lemon contrasting with the cheese mixture.

METRIC/IMPERIAL
For lining the pie dish :
25 g/1 oz butter
100 g/4 oz fine semi-sweet biscuit crumbs
For the filling :
75 g/3 oz butter
75 g/3 oz castor sugar
2 large or 3 small eggs
grated rind and juice of 1 lemon
350 g/12 oz cream or cottage cheese, sieved
2 tablespoons thick cream
lemon slices to decorate
Serves 4-6

Melt the butter and mix in the crumbs. Press against the sides and base of an 18-20 cm/7-8 inch pie dish.

Cream the butter and sugar, separate the eggs and add the egg yolks and the lemon rind to the creamed mixture. Then work in the cheese, the cream and the lemon juice, until the mixture forms a really smooth consistency.

Whisk the egg whites until stiff and fold into the mixture. Put into the crumb-lined dish and sprinkle the remaining crumbs as a border round the cheesecake.

Bake in a cool oven (140°C, 275°F, Gas Mark 1) until set, about 1¼ hours. Decorate with halved slices of lemon.

✻ This cheesecake freezes excellently. Use within 3 months.

Strawberry Shortcake

METRIC/IMPERIAL
75 g/3 oz plain flour
40 g/1½ oz cornflour
1 teaspoon baking powder
100 g/4 oz margarine
50 g/2 oz castor sugar
1 egg
For the filling and topping :
1 small punnet fresh strawberries
150 ml/¼ pint double cream
1 egg white
Serves 4-6

Sift the flour, cornflour and baking powder. Cream together the margarine and sugar until light and fluffy. Add the egg and beat in thoroughly.

Add the sifted flour, cornflour and baking powder and fold in lightly with a metal spoon.

Grease an 18-cm/7-inch deep sandwich or cake tin and line the bottom with a round of greased greaseproof paper. Place the mixture in the tin, smooth flat on top and bake on second shelf from the top of a moderately hot oven (190°C, 375°F, Gas Mark 5) for 25-30 minutes. Cool on a wire tray.

Cut the shortcake through the centre. Prepare the strawberries. Keep back about 8 of the best to decorate the top and slice the remainder.

Place the double cream in a bowl and whisk until stiff. Whisk the egg white until stiff. Fold the egg white into the cream. Mix half the cream with the sliced strawberries. Spread on to half of the shortcake. Place the other half on top.

Pile the remaining cream on top and decorate with a circle of strawberries.

✳ Freeze before filling and use within 3 months.

Rich Gingerbread

METRIC/IMPERIAL
150 g/5 oz butter or margarine
100 g/4 oz brown sugar
175 g/6 oz black treacle or golden syrup
1 tablespoon water
200 g/7 oz plain flour
1 teaspoon bicarbonate of soda
2 teaspoons ground ginger
1 teaspoon grated lemon rind
2 eggs

1 Put the butter, sugar, treacle and water into a pan and heat gently until the butter has melted.

2 Sift all the dry ingredients together. Pour the melted ingredients on to the dry mixture and beat hard until thoroughly mixed. Make sure no mixture is left in the pan.

3 Add the lemon rind and eggs and beat once again.

4 Pour into a greased and lined 18-cm/7-inch round cake tin. Bake in the centre of a moderate oven (160°C, 325°F, Gas Mark 3) for 1-1¼ hours. An oblong tin will take just under an hour.

Test by pressing gently in the centre of the cake. If no impression is left by your finger, the cake is cooked. Cool for about 30 minutes in the tin, then turn out carefully on to a wire tray. This gingerbread keeps well for several weeks in an airtight container.
✳ Can be frozen for up to 3 months.

1

2

3

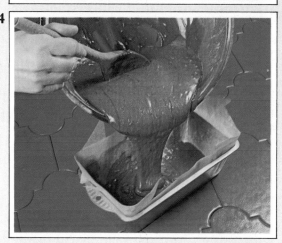

4

Choux Pastry

METRIC/IMPERIAL
150 ml/¼ pint water
25 g/1 oz margarine or butter
pinch of sugar
75 g/3 oz plain flour
2 whole eggs and yolk of 1 egg or
3 small eggs

Put the water, margarine or butter and sugar into a saucepan. Heat gently until the fat has melted. Bring quickly to the boil. Remove from the heat and stir in the flour all at once, beating well.

Return the pan to a low heat and cook very gently but thoroughly, beating all the time, until the mixture is dry enough to form a ball and leave the pan clean.

Once again remove the pan from the heat and allow to cool slightly. Gradually add the well-beaten eggs. Do this slowly to produce a perfectly smooth mixture. Use for cream buns and éclairs.

Éclairs

Insert a plain pipe, 1 cm/½ inch in diameter, into a piping bag. Half-fill the bag with choux pastry mixture, then pipe in narrow strips on to lightly greased baking trays.

Bake the éclairs in a hot oven (220°C, 425°F, Gas Mark 7) for 20-25 minutes. Open the door carefully after 15 minutes cooking and if the éclairs are browning rather quickly, lower the heat.

Take the éclairs out of the oven at the end of the cooking time and cool away from a draught. Split in half, or make a slit down the side. Fill with whipped cream and cover with coffee or chocolate glacé icing.

To make the coffee or chocolate glacé icing: blend 175 g/6 oz icing sugar and 1 teaspoon instant coffee powder or 2 teaspoons cocoa with a little warm water until smooth and the right consistency.

❋ Freeze unfilled. Use within 3 months and crisp for 2-3 minutes in the oven.

Profiteroles

Make choux pastry and either pipe or spoon the mixture on to a greased baking tray in rounds the size of a walnut. Allow room for them to expand.

Bake in a moderately hot oven (200°C, 400°F, Gas Mark 6) for 20-25 minutes, until well risen, puffed and crisp. Cool, split and fill with whipped cream.

Pile into a pyramid shape in one dish or individual dishes and serve with hot or cold chocolate sauce.

To make the chocolate sauce: melt 175 g/6 oz plain chocolate with 15 g/½ oz butter and 2 tablespoons water or milk in a bowl over a pan of hot water. Stir to blend the ingredients.

❋ Freeze as for éclairs.

Sponge Cake

METRIC/IMPERIAL
3 large eggs
100 g/4 oz castor sugar
75 g/3 oz flour (with plain flour use
½ teaspoon baking powder)
1 tablespoon hot water
25 g/1 oz butter or margarine, melted, if
the cake is to be kept a day or two
icing sugar to dust

1 Grease and flour, or grease and coat with equal quantities of flour and sugar, two 18-cm/7-inch sandwich tins. Put the eggs and sugar into a basin and whisk until the mixture is thick and the whisk leaves a trail. You will get a lighter result if not whisked over hot water.

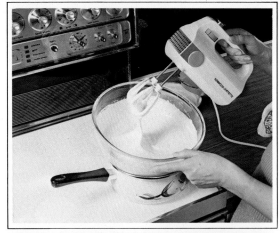

2 Using a metal spoon, carefully fold in the sifted flour with the baking powder, if used. Fold in the water and butter. Divide the mixture between the prepared tins and bake near the top of a moderately hot oven (190-200°C, 375-400°F, Gas Mark 5-6) for 10-15 minutes.

3 Test by pressing gently but firmly in the centre of the cakes. When firm they are cooked. Take out of the oven, leave to cool for a minute, tap the tins sharply then turn on to a wire tray. Cool away from a draught then sandwich together with jam. Dust the top with sifted icing sugar.

✳ The texture of this sponge seems to improve with freezing. Use within 3 months.

Variations
Chocolate sponge: as above, but omit 15 g/½ oz flour and add 15 g/½ oz cocoa powder. Fill with whipped cream and sprinkle with icing sugar.
Coffee sponge: as above, using 1 tablespoon coffee essence instead of hot water, or 1 teaspoon instant coffee powder dissolved in 3 teaspoons water. Fill with whipped cream and cover top and sides with coffee icing (see page 134). Press flaked almonds into the icing.

Basic Sweet Soufflé

METRIC/IMPERIAL
1 tablespoon cornflour
150 ml/¼ pint milk
3-4 eggs (4 eggs give a lighter soufflé, or
use yolks of 3 eggs and whites of 4)
15-25 g/½-1 oz butter
50 g/2 oz sugar
flavouring
1 tablespoon icing sugar

Serves 4

Blend the cornflour with a little of the milk
until smooth. Put the remaining milk into a
saucepan and bring to the boil over a
moderate heat. Pour over the blended
cornflour, return to the saucepan and bring
to the boil, stirring all the time. When
thick, remove from the heat.

Separate the egg yolks from the egg
whites. Stir the butter and sugar into the
sauce, then gradually beat in the egg yolks
with a wooden spoon. Add the flavouring.

Whisk the egg whites until really stiff and
fold into the sauce and egg yolk mixture
with a metal spoon. Put into a 1.25-litre/2-
pint soufflé dish, stand on a baking tray and
bake in the centre of a moderately hot oven
(190°C, 375°F, Gas Mark 5) for 25-35
minutes, until well risen and golden brown.

Dust the top of the soufflé with a tablespoon of sifted icing sugar before putting
on to the table; make sure the icing sugar is
ready before the soufflé is brought from the
oven otherwise the soufflé will subside.

Flavourings for Hot Soufflés

Chocolate: blend 50 g/2 oz melted plain
chocolate with the sauce or mix 15 g/½ oz
cocoa with the cornflour. Flavour with a
few drops of vanilla essence and 1 tablespoon double cream.
Coffee: use strong black coffee in place of
milk and add 2 tablespoons double cream to
the sauce.

Meringues

METRIC/IMPERIAL
2 egg whites
60 g/2 oz castor sugar plus 50 g/2 oz icing
sugar, sifted, or 110 g/4 oz castor sugar

Makes 8 complete meringues

Whisk the egg whites until stiff, fold in the
sugar gradually or whisk in half the sugar
and fold in the rest.

Pipe or pile small spoonfuls on to well
oiled greaseproof paper on a baking tray, or
use silicone paper.

Bake in a very cool oven (110-120°C,
225-250°F, Gas Mark ¼-½) for 2-3 hours,
depending on size, until crisp but still
white.

Lift from the paper with a palette knife,
cool, then store in airtight tins.

Sandwich together with whipped cream,
ice cream or fruit and cream, or butter
icing. Do not fill until nearly time to serve.

Pavlova

METRIC/IMPERIAL
4 egg whites
few drops of vanilla essence
225 g/8 oz castor sugar
1 teaspoon cornflour
1 teaspoon vinegar
300 ml/½ pint double cream
225 g/8 oz canned or fresh fruit

Serves 6-8

Draw on greaseproof paper an oval or round 20 cm/8 inches in diameter. Place on a greased baking tray and oil the paper.

Whisk the egg whites and vanilla essence until stiff. Gradually whisk in half the sugar then fold in the rest of the sugar, the cornflour and vinegar. Place in an icing bag fitted with a star pipe. Pipe round the pencil shape and over the entire centre. Pipe round the edge, building it up to form a wall.

Bake in a very cool oven (110°C, 225°F, Gas Mark ¼) for 3-4 hours until dry and crisp. Lift off the tray and paper whilst still warm.

Cool and store in an airtight tin. When required to serve, whip the cream and fill the meringue case with the cream and fruit.

Rough Puff Pastry

METRIC/IMPERIAL
225 g/8 oz plain flour
pinch of salt
175 g/6 oz fat, preferably half butter and
half lard
2 teaspoons lemon juice (optional)
6 tablespoons cold water

1 Sift the flour and salt into a mixing bowl. Cut the fat into small pieces and put into the flour. When the fat has been added, mix with the lemon juice and sufficient water to form a soft dough. *Do not rub the fat into the flour before adding the lemon juice and water* – it should remain in pieces.

2 Shake a little flour on to a pastry board and put the dough on this. Shape it into an oblong and roll lightly with a floured rolling pin into a long strip. Fold neatly in three. Seal the ends and 'rib' it. This means depressing the pastry with the rolling pin at intervals to give a corrugated effect and equalise the pressure of air. This ensures the pastry rising evenly. Give the pastry a half-turn and repeat the rolling and folding once more. Place in a polythene bag and allow to rest in a refrigerator or cold place for 20 minutes. Repeat the rolling and folding process twice more. Place in a polythene bag and chill before using.

✳ See Short Crust pastry, page 126.

Steak and Kidney Pie

METRIC/IMPERIAL
575-675 g/1¼-1½ lb stewing steak
2 lamb's kidneys or 100 g/4 oz ox kidney
1 tablespoon flour
salt and pepper
150 ml/¼ pint water or stock
225 g/8 oz rough puff pastry
beaten egg or milk to glaze

Serves 4-6

1 Cut the steak and kidney into small pieces and mix well. Roll in the seasoned flour. Stand a pie funnel in the centre of a 1-litre/1½-pint pie dish and fill with the meat. Pour on the water or stock. Roll out the pastry and cut a 2.5-cm/1-inch strip from the outer edge. Place on the moistened rim of the pie dish and brush with water.

2 Lift the remaining pastry on a rolling pin and cover the pie. Seal and knock up the edges. Flute with a knife. Use any scraps of pastry left to form leaves or a tassel or roses to decorate the pie. Brush the top of the pie with the beaten egg or milk, pressing the decoration in position. Make a tiny slit in the pastry over the pie funnel to allow the steam to escape. Bake in the centre of a hot oven (220°C, 425°F, Gas Mark 7) for 25-30 minutes, to enable the pastry to rise. Put a piece of greaseproof paper over the top of the pie, lower the heat to moderate (160°C, 325°F, Gas Mark 3) and cook for a further 1½ hours.

❄ Freeze uncooked for 3 months, cooked for 4 months.

Variation
The meat may be cooked first before covering with the pastry. Put the meat in a casserole and pour on the water or stock. Cook in a cool oven for 2 hours and set aside to cool. Then transfer the meat to a pie dish, cover with the pastry and bake the pie in a hot oven for 25-30 minutes only.

Flaky Pastry

METRIC/IMPERIAL
225 g/8 oz plain flour
pinch of salt
175 g/6 oz butter or margarine (or half
butter or margarine and half lard)
6-8 tablespoons cold water
2 teaspoons lemon juice

Sift the flour with the salt. Divide the fat into four. Rub one quarter into the flour in the usual way and mix to a soft dough with cold water and lemon juice. Knead lightly then roll out to an oblong shape. Now take the second portion of fat, divide it into small pieces and lay them evenly on two-thirds of the dough. Leave remaining third without fat. Take its two corners and fold back over second third so that the dough looks like an envelope with its flap open. Fold over the top end of the pastry, so closing the 'envelope'. Turn the pastry at right angles, seal the ends of the pastry and 'rib' it (see Rough puff pastry, page 152).

Repeat the process again, using the third portion of fat, folding and turning the pastry in the same way. Place in a polythene bag and rest in the refrigerator or cold place for 20 minutes. Repeat the rolling and folding process using the last portion of fat. Roll out and place in a polythene bag to chill before using.

Altogether, the pastry should have four foldings and four rollings, plus an extra roll at the end.

✳ See Short Crust pastry, page 126.

Sausage Rolls

METRIC/IMPERIAL
350 g/12 oz flaky pastry
350 g/12 oz sausagemeat or skinless
sausages
beaten egg or milk to glaze

*Makes 8 large or 16 medium or 32 cocktail
size sausage rolls*

Roll out the pastry thinly on a floured board. Cut into oblongs about 10 cm/ 4 inches wide and 25-30 cm/10-12 inches long.

Lay sausages or rolls of sausagemeat down the centre of the oblong. Dampen the edges of the pastry. Fold the edges together, pressing them securely together. Cut the strip into 4 equal lengths. Snip holes in the tops of the rolls with scissors or prick with a fork. Brush over with beaten egg or milk.

Bake in the centre of a hot oven (220°C, 425°F, Gas Mark 7) for 20-25 minutes, until a golden brown, turning the heat down after 12-15 minutes if necessary.

✳ Freeze uncooked for 3 months, cooked for 4 months.

in the refrigerator or cold place for 20 minutes. Repeat the rolling and folding process four times, resting the dough if it becomes sticky.

Always rest the dough in a cold place before rolling for the last time and before baking. Puff pastry should rise to 4-5 times its original thickness.

Vol-au-Vent Cases

These are ideal for so many occasions. Choose rough puff, flaky or puff pastry. Roll out until about 1 cm/$\frac{1}{2}$ inch in thickness for tiny cases but up to 2.5 cm/1 inch in thickness for large ones. For cocktail vol-au-vent cases, cut into rounds, about 3.5 cm/1$\frac{1}{2}$ inches in diameter, using a cutter dipped into cold water. Then take a smaller cutter 1.5 cm/$\frac{3}{4}$ inch in diameter and press through the pastry on top to a depth of 5 mm/$\frac{1}{4}$ inch. Place the pastry cases on a dampened baking tray and brush with beaten egg mixed with water.

Bake in a hot oven (220-230°C, 425-450°F, Gas Mark 7-8) for 8-10 minutes until crisp and golden brown. Using the point of a sharp knife, lift off the 'lids' and return the cases to the oven for a few minutes to dry out. Fill just before serving.

Puff Pastry

METRIC/IMPERIAL
225 g/8 oz plain flour
generous pinch of salt
6-8 tablespoons cold water
2 teaspoons lemon juice
225 g/8 oz butter or half butter and
half lard

Sift the flour and salt and mix to a soft dough with cold water and lemon juice. Knead well then roll to an oblong shape and place a neat block of fat in the centre of the pastry. Fold over the bottom section of the pastry, and then the top so that the fat is covered. Turn the dough at right angles, seal the edges and 'rib' (see Rough puff pastry, page 152). Roll out and fold the dough into an 'envelope' shape. Turn, seal the edges and 'rib' again.

Place in a polythene bag and leave to rest

Fillings

Fish: white fish, salmon or shellfish blended with a béchamel sauce.
Meat and poultry: ham and poultry blended with a béchamel sauce or any other savoury sauce.
Vegetable: either boil, or as with mushrooms, fry in butter, and blend with béchamel, cheese or white sauce.
Sweet: fruit mixed with cream.
❋ Freeze cases unfilled. Use uncooked cases within 4 months, cooked within 5-6 months.

Puddings and Desserts

Secrets of Success

If you consider the variety of puddings and desserts from which one can choose, it seems they cover a wide selection of flavours and textures, but have little in common from the point of view of cooking techniques.

In fact this is not true – one can group both hot puddings or cold desserts under basic headings:

Baking – this covers crumble mixtures, meringue-topped desserts, milk puddings, egg custards and pastry. The baking temperatures must vary according to the type of dish.

A crumble needs a moderate oven so the rubbed-in mixture crisps steadily.

Meringues are covered in the previous chapter on baking (page 150), and the principle of making a meringue-topped dessert is similar: the whisking of the egg whites, the thorough but correct method of incorporating the sugar and a slow to moderate temperature in baking, depending upon whether the pudding is to be served hot or cold.

Slow baking is the secret of a creamy milk pudding or egg custard. The latter should stand in a bain-marie (a container of water) to keep the custard smooth and prevent it curdling (separating). You must have a sufficiently low temperature for the egg custard, but it is equally important to time the baking carefully so the custard does not over-cook. Either *too high* a temperature or *too long* in the oven could cause curdling.

Steaming – ideal for cooking hot puddings, ranging from a light sponge to a traditional rich Christmas pudding. I am a great believer in steaming quickly for the first third of the cooking period, in the case of light puddings, for it does give a better texture. Take care the pan under the steamer is kept filled with boiling water throughout the cooking period.

Setting is not a cooking process, but an important stage in the making of many desserts using gelatine. Modern gelatines dissolve readily if you follow this procedure:

a) put the gelatine in a basin with a little of the cold liquid;

b) stand the basin over a pan of boiling water and leave until dissolved. Do not stir during this period. As soon as the gelatine has dissolved remove from over the boiling water. In some recipes you are told to soften the gelatine only then stir this into hot liquid.

If making a light dessert based upon gelatine which uses cream and egg whites, allow the gelatine mixture to stiffen slightly before incorporating the lightly whipped cream and stiffly whisked egg whites. This keeps them evenly blended and prevents them separating out.

Fruit Crumble

METRIC/IMPERIAL
450 g/1 lb fruit
sugar to taste
100 g/4 oz plain flour
50 g/2 oz butter or margarine
75 g/3 oz sugar

Serves 4

Put the fruit with the sugar and a very little water into a fairly large pie dish. Soft berry fruits, such as raspberries and black-currants, will need no water at all.
To make the topping: sift the flour and rub the butter into it. Add the sugar and sprinkle the crumbs evenly over the fruit, pressing down fairly firmly. This makes certain the crust can be cut into neat slices.

Bake in a moderately hot oven (190°C, 375°F, Gas Mark 5) for about 25 minutes until crisp and golden brown. Serve hot or cold.

❋ Freezes well for 3 months.

Apple Amber

METRIC/IMPERIAL
450-575 g/1-1¼ lb apples
100-150 g/4-5 oz sugar
2 eggs, separated

Serves 4

Simmer the apples with very little water and half of the sugar. When a thick, smooth pulp, add the beaten egg yolks. Pour into a dish and cook in a moderate oven (180°C, 350°F, Gas Mark 4) for 30 minutes.

Whisk the egg whites until very stiff, fold in the remaining sugar and pile on top of the apple mixture. Return to the oven and brown the meringue for 20 minutes if serving hot. If serving cold, place in a cool oven (150°C, 300°F, Gas Mark 2) for about 1 hour.

Queen of Puddings

METRIC/IMPERIAL
2 eggs, separated
100 g/4 oz sugar
300 ml/½ pint hot milk
50 g/2 oz fine cake or breadcrumbs
finely grated rind of 1 lemon
little jam

Serves 4

Beat the egg yolks with half the sugar. Pour on the hot milk. Put the crumbs and finely grated lemon rind into a basin and strain the egg and milk liquid over them. Put a little jam in the bottom of a pie dish and pour in the mixture.

Bake in a moderate oven (160°C, 325°F, Gas Mark 3) for 35-40 minutes, until firm. Spread jam over the top. Whisk the egg whites until stiff and fold in the remaining sugar. Spread over the jam. Return to the oven for about 20 minutes. Serve hot.

Crème Caramel

METRIC/IMPERIAL
75 g/3 oz castor sugar
3 tablespoons water
squeeze of lemon juice
2 whole eggs
2 egg yolks
2 tablespoons sugar
600 ml/1 pint milk

Serves 4

First make the caramel sauce. Put the 75 g/3 oz sugar, water and lemon juice into a small heavy pan, place over a low heat and allow the sugar to dissolve. The syrup must not come to the boil until all the sugar has dissolved. Bring to the boil and simmer rapidly until it is a deep golden colour. Remove from the heat and pour into a warmed soufflé dish, cake tin or dariole moulds, turning to coat the sides and the bottom evenly with the caramel.

Lightly beat the eggs and sugar with a fork, heat the milk to just under boiling point and pour on to the beaten eggs. Stir and strain on to the caramel. Stand in a baking tin with enough hot water round it to come halfway up the sides, cover with a piece of buttered paper or foil and bake in a cool oven (150°C, 300°F, Gas Mark 2) for about 1 hour or until quite set. Dariole moulds need only 40-45 minutes.

Allow the custard to cool before turning it out.

Bread and Butter Pudding

METRIC/IMPERIAL
2 eggs
sugar
450 ml/¾ pint warm milk
2 large slices bread
little butter
50 g/2 oz dried fruit

Serves 4

Whisk the eggs with a fork, add 1 teaspoon sugar and the warm milk – the milk must not boil or it will curdle the eggs.

Remove the crusts from the bread and butter lightly. Cut into neat squares or triangles and arrange in a pie dish. Add the dried fruit and pour the egg custard over the top. Allow to stand for 30 minutes.

Sprinkle the top with a little sugar and bake in a moderate oven (160°C, 325°F, Gas Mark 3) for about 1 hour. If the pudding appears to be cooking too quickly after 40 minutes, lower the heat.

Treacle Tart

METRIC/IMPERIAL
175 g/6 oz short crust pastry
(see page 126)
2-3 tablespoons golden syrup or black treacle
2 tablespoons soft breadcrumbs

Serves 4

Line a 20-cm/8-inch pie plate or flan tin with the pastry. Either prick the pastry well with a fork or line with greaseproof paper and place dried beans on it to weigh down the pastry. Bake 'blind' in a hot oven (220°C, 425°F, Gas Mark 7) for 10 minutes. While the treacle or syrup can be put into the uncooked pastry, baking 'blind' is a better method as it gives crisper pastry.

Put the warmed syrup or treacle over the half-cooked pastry, cover with the bread-crumbs and return to the centre of the oven for a further 10-15 minutes.

✳ Freeze for 3 months.

Light Fritter Batter

METRIC/IMPERIAL
100 g/4 oz plain flour
pinch of salt
2 eggs, separated
150 ml/¼ pint milk and water

Sift the flour and salt, beat in the egg yolks and milk and water. Whisk the egg whites until stiff and fold in just before cooking the fritters.

Apple Fritters

METRIC/IMPERIAL
3 large cooking apples
1 tablespoon flour
1 tablespoon sugar (optional)
light fritter batter
oil for deep frying
sugar for coating
lemon slices to decorate

Serves 4

Peel and core the apples and slice fairly thinly (this makes sure that they may be adequately cooked without over-browning the outside). Dust with flour (the sugar may be added to the flour).

Heat the oil to 180°C/350°F (see page 45). Dip the fritters in the batter and fry steadily until crisp and golden brown. Drain on kitchen paper and sprinkle with sugar. Decorate with slices of lemon.

For other fruit fritters choose:
Fresh: fresh firm bananas, firm ripe apricots or plums, greengages, small ripe pears (halved and cored), rings of pineapple.
Canned: well-drained canned pineapple rings, halved peaches, pears.

Beignets Soufflés

METRIC/IMPERIAL
choux pastry (see page 146)
2 teaspoons sugar
½ teaspoon vanilla essence
oil for deep frying
castor sugar for coating
jam sauce (see page 89)

Serves 4

Make the choux pastry as given in the basic recipe, and beat in the sugar and vanilla essence with the eggs. Heat the oil to 180°C/350°F (see page 45). Drop small spoonfuls of the choux pastry into the hot oil and fry until golden brown. Drain on kitchen paper. Sprinkle with sugar and serve with hot jam sauce.

Soufflé Omelette

METRIC/IMPERIAL
2 large eggs
1 tablespoon water, milk or cream
sugar to taste
butter

Serves 1

Separate the egg yolks and whites. Beat the yolks with the water, milk or cream. Add sugar to taste. Whisk the egg whites until stiff and fold in. Heat a little butter in the omelette pan, add the eggs and allow to cook for 2 minutes. Because this is so thick it is difficult to get it cooking quickly enough from the bottom, so put the soufflé omelette under a preheated grill or in the oven when it is reasonably set at the bottom. In this way it will cook quickly without toughening the eggs.

When the egg mixture is set on top, add the filling, fold and serve immediately.

Sweet fillings
Banana and nut: heat sliced banana in a little butter with chopped walnuts or hazelnuts. Sprinkle with sugar.
Jam: add a little sugar to taste before cooking, then fill the omelette with hot jam. Fold and dust with sifted icing sugar.

Steamed Sponge Pudding

METRIC/IMPERIAL
75 g/3 oz butter or margarine
75 g/3 oz castor sugar
2 eggs
100 g/4 oz self-raising flour
1 tablespoon milk

Serves 4

Cream the butter or margarine and sugar together until soft and light. Add the eggs gradually, then fold in the sifted flour and the milk. Grease a 1-litre/1½-pint pudding basin and pour the mixture into this.

Cover with greaseproof paper or foil and put in a steamer over a saucepan of boiling water. Steam over rapidly boiling water for 30 minutes, then steam steadily for a further 45 minutes–1 hour. Turn out on to a hot dish and serve immediately with any sweet sauce.

❋ Freeze the uncooked mixture for 1 month, the cooked pudding for 3 months.

Chocolate Sauce

METRIC/IMPERIAL
3 teaspoons cornflour
3 teaspoons cocoa
300 ml/½ pint milk
1 tablespoon sugar
vanilla essence
15 g/½ oz butter

Serves 4

Blend the cornflour and cocoa with a little milk. Heat the remainder of the milk, and when nearly boiling pour on to the blended mixture. Return to the heat and cook, stirring, for 2 minutes. Add the sugar, a few drops of vanilla essence and the butter.

Lemon Sauce

METRIC/IMPERIAL
2 lemons
2 teaspoons arrowroot or cornflour
50 g/2 oz sugar, or to taste
finely grated rind of 1 lemon

Measure the juice from the lemons and make up to 300 ml/½ pint with water. Mix the arrowroot or cornflour to a smooth paste with a little of the liquid. Heat the remainder in a saucepan, add the sugar and stir until dissolved. Pour over the blended arrowroot and return to the pan. Cook until the sauce thickens and becomes clear, stirring constantly. Stir in the grated lemon rind and pour into a jug or sauceboat.

Orange sauce: use either 2 large oranges, or you have a better flavoured sauce if you use 1 good-sized orange and 1 small lemon. Continue as above.

Golden Syrup Sauce

METRIC/IMPERIAL
3 tablespoons golden syrup
grated rind and juice of 1 lemon
150 ml/¼ pint water

Put the syrup into a saucepan together with the grated rind and juice of the lemon. Add the water and heat gently for a few minutes.

Fruit Suet Pudding

cook the custard in a basin, that balances safely over a pan of hot water, or if the heat on the top of the cooker can be turned down very low, cook in an ordinary saucepan, but the custard must not be allowed to boil otherwise it will curdle.

METRIC/IMPERIAL
225 g/8 oz suet crust pastry (see Steak and Kidney Pudding, page 78)
450 g/1 lb prepared fruit
50-75 g/2-3 oz sugar

Serves 4

Make the pastry and line the basin as described on page 79. Fill with the prepared fruit, sugar and about 2 tablespoons water, the amount depending on the juiciness of the fruit. Roll out the remaining pastry and press over the top of the pudding.

Cover with greased greaseproof paper or foil and steam over boiling water for about 2 hours, making sure the water really does boil. Turn out on to a hot dish and serve with cream or egg custard sauce.

❄ Freezes well for 5 months.

Egg Custard Sauce

METRIC/IMPERIAL
1 large egg or 2 egg yolks (for a thicker sauce)
15-25 g/½-1 oz sugar
300 ml/½ pint warm milk

Serves 4

Beat the egg or egg yolks and the sugar together. Add the warmed milk, beating well. Strain the mixture into the top of a double saucepan with hot *but not boiling* water underneath.

Cook slowly, stirring from time to time with a wooden spoon, until the mixture is sufficiently thick to coat the back of the spoon. If no double saucepan is available,

Christmas Pudding

METRIC/IMPERIAL
450 g/1 lb stoned or seedless raisins
350 g/12 oz sultanas
350 g/12 oz currants
100 g/4 oz mixed candied peel
50 g/2 oz blanched almonds
50 g/2 oz flour
2 teaspoons ground mixed spice
1 teaspoon ground cinnamon
½ teaspoon grated nutmeg
225 g/8 oz white or brown sugar
225 g/8 oz fresh white breadcrumbs
grated rind of 1 lemon
100 g/4 oz shredded suet
4 eggs
150 ml/¼ pint whisky or old ale or milk or
orange juice

Serves 14-16

Mix together the raisins, sultanas, currants, peel and almonds. Sift the flour and spices and add to the fruit mixture with the sugar, breadcrumbs, lemon rind and suet. Beat the eggs into the mixture with the whisky or other liquid. Stir well. Leave overnight if desired, then stir again, and wish.

Turn the mixture into greased pudding basins, either one 2.25-litre/4-pint, two 1.25-litre/2-pint or four small basins. Cover first with greaseproof paper and then with foil, or with a paste made by blending flour and water. Steam or boil for 4-8 hours, depending on size. Uncover and leave to cool. Re-cover with fresh grease-proof paper and foil and store in a cool, dry place. Christmas pudding keeps without freezing.

On Christmas Day, steam or boil for a further 3 hours. Serve with brandy butter or lightly whipped and sweetened cream.

Brandy Butter

METRIC/IMPERIAL
100 g/4 oz butter
150 g/5 oz icing sugar, sifted
½ teaspoon vanilla essence
1-2 tablespoons brandy

Serves 4-6

Cream the butter until light and fluffy, then gradually beat in the sifted icing sugar. Add the vanilla and sufficient brandy to give a good flavour. Continue beating until it is the consistency of whipped cream and pile or pipe into a pyramid shape on a small dish. Chill well.

Preparing Fruit for Desserts and Fruit Salads

Always remove the white pith from oranges and grapefruit, pips and stones from other fruit. Oranges and grapefruit are best peeled with a sharp fruit knife, so that the pith is removed at the same time. Special cherry stoners can be bought, or you can use the bent end of a fine new hairpin. To cut a pineapple, make slanting cuts downwards, between the eyes. Remove the eyes and skin, then slice across with a stainless steel knife and remove the core with an apple corer. To peel fresh peaches, place in a bowl and pour boiling water over them. Leave for a minute when the skin can be peeled away easily.

For the sugar syrup simmer 100 g/4 oz sugar in 150 ml/¼ pint water for about 3 minutes. Add a few drops of Angostura bitters. The thinly peeled rind of a lemon can also be added. Pour the syrup over the fruit and chill.

If bananas, apples or pears are to be included, toss in a little lemon juice to prevent discoloration.

These fruits pair deliciously: grapefruit and pineapple – orange and raspberries – plums and bananas – apricots with dates and coconut – canned apple sauce with mandarin sections and chopped ginger.

Sprigs of mint and borage make fragrant decorations.

Fruit Salad

The flavour of a fruit salad is much improved if it is made an hour or two before serving. Marinate the fruit in a sprinkling of sugar syrup – and for a special occasion add wine, cider or ginger ale. A dash or two of Angostura bitters is a chef's trick to develop the fruit flavour.

Apple Fool

METRIC/IMPERIAL
150 ml/¼ pint thick sweetened custard
(make as directed with custard powder)
450 g/1 lb apples
2 tablespoons water
25-50 g/1-2 oz sugar
generous squeeze of lemon juice
150 ml/¼ pint double cream, whipped
To decorate:
glacé cherries
angelica pieces

Make the custard and allow to cool. Peel, core and slice the apples. Put into a saucepan with the water and sugar. Cook gently so they do not burn.

When the apples are smooth, beat well with a wooden spoon, adding the lemon juice. Allow to cool. When the apple and custard are both cold, beat them together or liquidise and fold in the whipped cream. Spoon into four glasses, chill and decorate with cherries and angelica.

Other fruit fools
Most fruit can be served as a fruit fool, but soft fruit such as strawberries need no cooking, just mashing or sieving then sweetening. Other fruits particularly good in fruit fools are:

Gooseberries and blackcurrants: these should be pressed through a sieve, after cooking, to remove the skins.

Plums: stone and halve before cooking so that the minimum of water is required.

Rhubarb: cook with the minimum of water, sieve if wished.

Lemon Cream Mould

METRIC/IMPERIAL
15 g/½ oz powdered gelatine
75 g/3 oz castor sugar
150 ml/¼ pint hot water
450 ml/¾ pint milk
juice of 2 lemons
grated rind of 1 lemon
To decorate:
double cream, whipped
glacé cherry

Serves 6

Dissolve the gelatine in the hot water, then stir in the sugar. Cool slightly and mix into the milk. Whisk in the lemon juice and the grated lemon rind. As soon as the mixture starts to set, pour into a mould, previously rinsed with cold water.

When set, turn out and decorate with whipped double cream and a glacé cherry.

Ice Cream

METRIC/IMPERIAL
300 ml/½ pint egg custard sauce (see page
166), made with 2 egg yolks only
flavouring (see below)
25-50 g/1-2 oz icing sugar, sifted
300 ml/½ pint double cream
2 egg whites

Serves 4-6

1 Make the custard sauce and cover with a sheet of dampened greaseproof paper to prevent a skin forming while cooling. Add the flavouring and sugar.

2 Lightly whip the cream and fold into the custard mixture.

3 Spoon into the freezing trays and freeze for 35-40 minutes, until the mixture is beginning to stiffen, then remove from the trays into a cold bowl. Whisk well.

4 Whisk the egg whites and fold in. Return to the freezing trays and freeze until firm.

✳ Freezes well for up to 3 months.

To flavour
Fruit: use 150 ml/¼ pint mashed or sieved fresh bananas, strawberries, etc., or a smooth purée from canned or fresh fruit.
Chocolate: add 25 g/1 oz cocoa or chocolate powder to the custard.
Vanilla: add 1 teaspoon vanilla essence to the custard.

Lemon Sorbet

METRIC/IMPERIAL
2 eggs
rind and juice of 2 large lemons
300 ml/½ pint water
75 g/3 oz sugar

Serves 4

Separate the eggs. Peel strips of lemon rind from the fruit and simmer the rind with the water for 7-8 minutes. Strain the liquid. Beat the egg yolks with the sugar and pour over the liquid. Add the lemon juice. Freeze in the ice-making compartment of the refrigerator until thickening slightly.

Whisk the egg whites until stiff and stir into the slightly frozen sorbet. Return to the ice-making compartment and leave until firm.

❋ Keeps well in a freezer for 3 months.

Peach Melba

METRIC/IMPERIAL
2 large ripe peaches
4 portions ice cream
little whipped cream to decorate
(optional)
For the melba sauce:
1 teaspoon cornflour or arrowroot
2 tablespoons water
100-175 g/4-6 oz fresh raspberries
sugar to taste
3 tablespoons redcurrant or apple jelly
2 tablespoons brandy (optional)

Serves 4

First prepare the sauce. Blend the cornflour or arrowroot with the water. Put all the ingredients into a saucepan and heat gently until the jelly has melted and the mixture is clear. Rub through a sieve and add the brandy if wished. (When fresh raspberries are out of season, use frozen or canned raspberries and the syrup from these instead of water and sugar to taste). Set aside to cool.

Skin the peaches; it may be necessary to put these for about ½ minute into boiling water, then lift into cold water to remove the skin. Halve and remove the stones. Slice if wished.

Put into glasses and top with ice cream and the cold sauce. Pipe a little whipped cream on top if wished.

Baked Alaska

METRIC/IMPERIAL
1 sponge cake (see page 148)
450 g/1 lb fresh or canned fruit
1 (500-ml/17.6-fl oz) block ice cream
5 egg whites
150-275 g/6-10 oz castor sugar, or to taste

Place the sponge cake on an ovenproof serving dish. Cover with fresh or canned drained fruit and place the block of ice cream on top of the fruit.

Whisk the egg whites until very stiff. Add half the sugar and whisk until as stiff as before. Gently fold in the remaining sugar. Pile or pipe the meringue over the ice cream to cover it completely.

Bake in a very hot oven (240°C, 475°F, Gas Mark 9) for 3-5 minutes. Serve at once.

Yeast Cookery

Secrets of Success

There has been a great upsurge in yeast cookery during the past years. Making your own bread or buns is neither as difficult nor as time-consuming as imagined and the results are excellent, providing you follow a few basic instructions.

The choice of ingredients is very important. Yeast, whether fresh or dehydrated (dried), is the ingredient which makes the bread, or other dough, rise. Baking powder, therefore, is unnecessary.

When buying fresh yeast check it is in perfect condition; it should be putty-coloured, slightly crumbly so that it creams easily, and it should have a pleasant smell. Fresh yeast can be stored in a refrigerator for 4-5 days or even up to 3 weeks if wrapped loosely in a polythene bag. Fresh yeast, divided into small portions and wrapped well, can be frozen for up to 6 weeks. When using frozen yeast leave at room temperature for at least 30 minutes before using, or coarsely grate the frozen yeast to help defrosting.

You will find storage time for dried yeast on the packets or tins. This is generally about 6 months. Store in a cool dry place. You will always use half the amount of dried yeast in any recipe that only gives the

amount of fresh yeast. On page 176 are full directions for using both dried and fresh yeast in a recipe.

Choose the right flour. You will see that strong flour or plain flour are given. Strong flour is better for bread-making and similar recipes. With its higher gluten content than ordinary flours it produces a yeast dough that rises better and has a finer texture. If strong flour is not available substitute plain flour.

When preparing yeast doughs keep the ingredients warm – but not too hot.

Kneading – an essential part of making a yeast dough. With the base of the palm, i.e. the 'heel', of the hand, press down on the dough and away from the body to stretch the dough. Fold the dough back towards you then press away again. You can tell if the dough is insufficiently kneaded; flour your forefinger and make an impression in the dough. If this comes out then the dough has been kneaded enough; if it stays in, then continue kneading.

Rising – the time taken for the dough to double in size will vary according to whether it is put in a cool or a warm place to rise.

Knocking back – when the dough has risen it has to be put on a floured surface and kneaded again until it regains its original size. This is known as 'knocking back'.

Proving – the word used to describe the dough rising for the second time after being knocked back.

Baking – oven temperatures are important. There must be sufficient heat to kill the yeast so the dough ceases to rise, but obviously the oven must not be too hot or it will over-brown the outside of the bread or buns before the inside is cooked.

Basic White Bread

METRIC/IMPERIAL

675 g/1½ lb strong or plain white flour
1 teaspoon salt
15 g/½ oz lard
15 g/½ oz fresh yeast or 2 teaspoons dried yeast and 1 teaspoon sugar
450 ml/¾ pint warm water (43°C/110°F)

Makes 1 large loaf or 2 small loaves or 18 rolls

1 Sift the flour and salt and rub in the lard. Blend the fresh yeast and water or sprinkle the dried yeast over the water and sugar and leave until frothy (the 'sponge' breaks through), about 10 minutes.

2 Mix the dry ingredients with the yeast liquid, using a wooden spoon. Work to a fine dough with the hand, adding extra flour if needed, until the sides of the bowl are clean.

  Turn the dough on to a lightly floured board or table and knead thoroughly to stretch and develop the dough. To do this, fold the dough towards you then push down and away with the base of the palm of the hand.

  Continue until the dough feels firm and elastic and no longer sticky, about 10 minutes.

3 Shape the dough into a ball. Place in a lightly greased large polythene bag loosely tied or a large saucepan with a lid, or place back into the bowl and cover with a teacloth.

4 Leave to rise until doubled in size and the dough springs back when pressed with a floured finger. You can choose the rising time to fit in with the day's plans.

Quick rise: 45 minutes-1 hour in a warm place.
Slow rise: 2 hours at average room temperature.
Overnight rise: up to 12 hours in a cold larder or room, or up to 24 hours in a refrigerator. Refrigerator-risen dough must be returned to room temperature before shaping – leave for about 20 minutes.

5 Turn the risen dough on to a lightly floured board or table. Flatten firmly with the knuckles to knock out air bubbles, then knead to make the dough firm and ready for shaping. When kneading or shaping bread, use only a little flour. Too much flour spoils the colour of the crust.

6 For a large loaf, grease and warm a 1-kg/2-lb loaf tin. Shape the dough into an oblong the same width as the tin. Fold into three and turn over so the seam is underneath. Smooth over the top, tuck in the ends and place in the tin. For 2 small loaves divide the dough into two and shape as above. Place in two warmed greased 0.5-kg/1-lb loaf tins. For 18 rolls, lightly grease one or two baking trays. Divide the dough into 18 equal pieces. Roll each piece into a ball or chosen shape, using the palm of the hand lightly. Place the rolls on a baking tray about 2.5 cm/1 inch apart. To 'prove', or rise again, either cover the tins with a cloth or slip into polythene bags. Leave to rise until the dough comes to the top of the tins, or the rolls are double their size.
Quick rise: rolls 15 minutes; breads 30-40 minutes in a warm place.
Slow rise: rolls 30 minutes; bread 1-1½ hours.
Refrigerator: rolls 6-8 hours or overnight; bread up to 16 hours.

To bake the dough, remove the polythene or cloths. Put into a hot oven (220°C, 425°F, Gas Mark 7 for bread, 230°C, 450°F, Gas Mark 8 for rolls). Bake a large loaf for about 40 minutes; smaller loaves for about 30 minutes; rolls for 12-15 minutes. The heat may be reduced to moderate if the loaves seem to be browning too much.

To test if cooked, the loaves should have shrunk from the sides of the tin and sound hollow when tapped underneath with the knuckles.

✳ Freeze cooked bread for up to 6 weeks. The uncooked yeast dough can be frozen for up to 2 months. Knead but do not put to rise before freezing. It is advisable to increase the yeast by 50% if freezing uncooked dough. Always leave to defrost then stand at room temperature.

Variations on Basic White Bread

Wholemeal bread: use all stone ground or wholemeal flour. You will need appreciably more liquid. The dough should be quite soft, so instead of kneading it, beat it with a wooden spoon to get a better result.

Fruit bread: add 100-175 g/4-6 oz mixed dried fruit to the flour, etc.

Malt bread: add 75 g/3 oz Ovaltine to the flour.

Milk bread: use milk instead of water. Skimmed milk makes a lighter bread; full cream milk a richer one.

Cheese Bread

METRIC/IMPERIAL
150 ml/¼ pint milk
50 g/2 oz lard or margarine
1-1½ teaspoons salt
25 g/1 oz fresh yeast
1 teaspoon sugar
just over 150 ml/¼ pint tepid water
675 g/1½ lb strong or plain flour
generous shake of pepper
100 g/4 oz Cheddar cheese, finely grated
1 egg
small knob of butter

Makes 1 large loaf or 2 small loaves

Heat the milk with half the lard and salt, then allow to cool slightly. Cream the yeast with the sugar, add the tepid water and the milk mixture. Sift the flour and pepper together. Rub in the rest of the lard. Add the cheese, egg and yeast liquid. Knead together until smooth. Allow to rise, as basic white bread.

Turn out and knead again. Form into one large or two small loaves. Put into one 1-kg/2-lb or two 0.5-kg/1-lb warmed and greased loaf tins and leave to rise again for about 20 minutes. Brush with a little melted butter to give a shiny crust. Bake in a hot oven (220°C, 425°F, Gas Mark 7) for 15 minutes, then lower the heat to moderately hot (190°C, 375°F, Gas Mark 5) for a further 15-20 minutes for the small loaves or 30-40 minutes for the large loaf.

Pizza

METRIC/IMPERIAL
15 g/½ oz fresh yeast
300 ml/½ pint tepid water
1 teaspoon sugar
450 g/1 lb strong or plain flour
½-1 teaspoon salt
4 tablespoons olive oil
450 g/1 lb tomatoes or 1 (396-g/14-oz) can
tomatoes
1 clove garlic, chopped
salt and pepper
100 g/4 oz Cheddar or Parmesan cheese,
grated
1 (56-g/2-oz) can anchovy fillets
few black olives

Dissolve the yeast in the tepid water and sugar. Sift the flour and salt, add 1 table-spoon of olive oil then the dissolved yeast. Knead until the dough is smooth. Allow to rise, as basic white bread.

Peel and chop the tomatoes, or drain canned tomatoes, and put them in a pan with the remaining oil and the garlic. Season with salt and pepper and simmer gently for 30 minutes. When the dough has risen, knead lightly then roll it out fairly thinly to a 25-cm/10-inch round and place on an oiled baking tray or in a large flan dish. Cover with the tomato mixture, sprinkle over the grated cheese and arrange anchovy strips and black olives on top.

Bake in the centre of a hot oven (220°C, 425°F, Gas Mark 7) for 20-25 minutes. Serve hot.

Plain Yeast Buns

METRIC/IMPERIAL
15 g/½ oz fresh yeast
25-50 g/1-2 oz sugar
250 ml/8 fl oz tepid milk or milk and water
350 g/12 oz strong or plain flour
generous pinch of salt
25 g/1 oz margarine or fat

Cream the yeast with a teaspoon of the sugar. Add the tepid liquid and a sprinkling of flour. Put into a warm place until the sponge breaks through.

Meanwhile sift the flour and salt into a warm bowl, rub in the margarine or fat and add the sugar. When ready work in the yeast liquid and knead thoroughly. Allow to rise, as basic white bread (see page 176).

Knead again until smooth and shape into desired shape. Cook near the top of a hot oven (220°C, 425°F, Gas Mark 7) for 10-15 minutes, depending upon size.

The buns can be split and filled with clotted cream and jam as Devonshire splits, or topped with a little glacé icing.

✳ As for basic white bread.

Fruit Buns

METRIC/IMPERIAL
15 g/½ oz fresh yeast
25g/1 oz sugar to glaze
250 ml/8 fl oz tepid milk or milk and water
350 g/12 oz strong or plain flour
generous pinch of salt
25 g/1 oz margarine
50-100 g/2-4 oz dried fruit
25-50 g/1-2 oz chopped candied peel
25 g/1 oz sugar to glaze
1 tablespoon water

Cream the yeast with a teaspoon of the sugar. Add the tepid liquid and a sprinkling of flour. Put into a warm place until the sponge breaks through.

Meanwhile sift the flour and salt into a warm bowl, rub in the margarine and add the sugar, fruit and peel. When ready, work in the yeast liquid and knead thoroughly. Allow to rise, as basic white bread (see page 176).

Knead the dough again. Form into round buns, prove for 15 minutes on a warm tray and bake near the top of a hot oven (220°C, 425°F, Gas Mark 7) for 10 minutes. Mix the sugar with a tablespoon of water and the moment the buns come from the oven, brush with this to give an attractive glaze.

Savarin

METRIC/IMPERIAL
100 g/4 oz plain flour
7 g/¼ oz fresh yeast or 1 teaspoon dried
yeast
1 teaspoon sugar
4 tablespoons tepid milk
50 g/2 oz butter or margarine
2 eggs
For the syrup:
50 g/2 oz sugar
150 ml/¼ pint water
1½-2 tablespoons rum
To decorate:
150 ml/¼ pint double cream
canned or fresh fruit

1 Put the flour in a warm basin. Cream the yeast with the sugar in a mixing bowl and add the tepid milk. Or sprinkle the dried yeast on to the milk, adding the sugar. Sprinkle on a little flour and leave in a warm place until the sponge breaks through.

2 Melt the butter or margarine. Add to the rest of the flour with all the other ingredients and the yeast liquid and beat well. Pour into a well-greased and floured 18-20 cm/7-8 inch ring tin.

3 Cover and allow to rise in a warm place for about 25 minutes, or until risen to the top of the tin. Bake in the centre of a hot oven (220°C, 425°F, Gas Mark 7) for about 30 minutes, reducing the heat slightly after 20 minutes if becoming too brown.

4 Meanwhile make the syrup. Dissolve the sugar in the water and simmer gently for a few minutes. Add the rum. Turn the cake out of the tin, prick while hot with a fine knitting needle or skewer and pour over the syrup. When cold, decorate with piped cream and canned or fresh fruit.

Wise Housekeeping

A Well Planned Store Cupboard

If your store cupboard is carefully planned and well stocked, you should be able to produce meals easily without rushing out to shop. These are some of the foods which provide the basis for good meals.

Arrowroot – for thickening fruit syrups.

Breadcrumbs – dried, for coating food.

Cheese – processed, although not as useful as Cheddar etc., can be used in cooking.

Cocoa and/or chocolate powder – for cooking and drinks.

Coffee – ground and instant. Keep ground coffee in a tightly sealed container so it does not lose flavour.

Cornflour – for quick thickening of sauces and in some baking. Use half the amount of cornflour if replacing flour in a sauce or gravy.

Custard powder – for sauces.

Dried fruit – mostly pre-washed today. If washing fruit, dry for 48 hours before using in cakes.

Essences – almond and vanilla the most useful.

Fish – anchovies, salmon, sardines, tuna.

Flour – if you do a lot of baking have plain (plus baking powder); self-raising; and strong flour. You may like all white flour, or some white and some wholemeal.

Fruit – have several cans of different fruits. Apple purée is a good stand-by for sauces if you do not freeze your own apples.

Glacé fruits – not essential, but glacé cherries are useful for decoration.

Golden syrup – for cooking.

Honey – for eating and cooking.

Mayonnaise – or salad dressing.

Meat – some useful canned meats and meat products are: corned beef, ham, stewing steak, tongue.

Milk – dried and/or evaporated – the latter can take the place of cream in some recipes.

Milk puddings – in cans, and some of the quick packet desserts to use with milk.

Oil – for frying and for salads.

Pasta – various shapes, e.g. lasagne, macaroni, spaghetti, etc.

Preserves – jam, marmalade, redcurrant jelly.

Rice – round for puddings, and long grain for savoury dishes.

Sauces – such as soy and Worcestershire.

Soups – choose those that could be used as a sauce in an emergency.

Spices and herbs – see separate paragraphs.

Stock cubes – to use in sauces, stews and soups.

Sugar – castor sugar for light cakes and puddings; granulated sugar for cooking fruit, sweetening sauces, etc.; various brown sugars such as demerara, a light brown sugar used for melted mixtures such as gingerbread, and moist brown sugar which gives the best result in rich cakes and recipes such as Christmas pudding; icing sugar for decoration; cube sugar for beverages.

Tomato purée – in a tube or can.

Vegetables – these will depend upon whether you have a freezer as frozen vegetables have a better flavour than canned. Also stock dried vegetables.

Vinegars – malt and wine or cider.

Choice of Herbs

There is an almost endless variety of herbs that can be stored in dried form or in the freezer when the fresh herbs are not available. The most useful are:

Basil, bay leaves, celery seeds and salt, chives, dill, fennel, garlic or garlic salt, lemon balm, marjoram and wild marjoram (oregano), mint, parsley, rosemary, sage, tarragon, thyme (ordinary and lemon).

If freezing herbs: chop the herbs and pack in small containers, or freeze in water in ice trays. When frozen, remove from the tray and pack. You can then add the herbs to a dish when cooking.

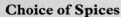

Choice of Spices

There are many more spices than those given below, but these are the most useful – they are mainly used in baking, but sometimes in savoury dishes:

Allspice, caraway, cinnamon, cloves, coriander (used mainly in curries), curry powder and paste, ginger, mustards (English and French), nutmeg, pepper (black, white and peppercorns), saffron, turmeric.

A Well Stocked Freezer

It is difficult to specify exactly how everyone should fill their freezer, for each family will use it in a slightly different way. Some people 'bulk buy' large quantities of various prepared foods, vegetables and fruits. Other people buy large quantities of meat at economical prices.

I feel the ideal way of filling a freezer is not only to save money by wise shopping, but to save time by cooking larger quantities of certain dishes, and freezing these, ready for future occasions. If you have a well stocked freezer you should be able to produce a meal with little effort.

Storage times for various foods and prepared dishes are given throughout this book, so I will simply summarise the kind of foods you can store – I have given these in the order one would consider them in a menu.

Hors d'oeuvre – pâtés, fruit juices.

Soups and stocks.

Fish – uncooked and prepared dishes.

Meat, poultry and game – uncooked and prepared dishes, including meat pies and puddings.

Stuffings – freeze separately from fish, meat or poultry.

Savoury dishes with pasta and rice, some cheese dishes, savoury spreads, sandwiches, sandwich fillings.

Sauces, or various foods in sauces.

Puddings and desserts – including pies, puddings, fruits and fruit purées of all kinds, ice creams, sorbets.

Pastry – uncooked, and in various cooked forms.

Vegetables and herbs – it is useful to have some cooked vegetable dishes as well as 'blanched' but uncooked vegetables.

Baked goods, such as bread and cakes.

A Well Stocked Refrigerator

As well as storing milk, cream, fats of all kinds, cheese (bring this out of the refrigerator an hour before serving), use the refrigerator for foods you intend to consume within a few days such as meats, salads, cold desserts. Keep food covered to prevent drying or intermingling of smells.

Storage Life of Canned Foods

There is a belief that canned foods can be stored for an indefinite period. This is not true and the following times are recommended as the *maximum* period.

Fruits – mostly 2 years, except prunes and rhubarb – 1 year; blackberries, gooseberries, plums, blackcurrants, raspberries and strawberries – 18 months.

Vegetables – 2 years, except new potatoes – 18 months.

Fish in sauce – 2 years; in oil – 5 years.

Meat – solid pack cold meat products – 5 years; hot meat products (stewed steak, etc.) 2 years.

Soups – 2 years.

Milk products, including milk puddings – 1 year.

Pasta products – 2 years.

Puddings – 2 years.

Index